Too Hard for God?

By the same author:
Streams in the Sahara
Share your Faith with a Muslim
Into Action

Too Hard for God?

C. R. Marsh

**with Postscript
by Daisy Marsh**

OM
publishing

British Library Cataloguing in Publication Data

A catalogue record for this book is available from the
British Library

ISBN 1-85078-362-4

Cover Design by Mainstream, Lancaster
Typeset by WestKey Limited, Falmouth, Cornwall
Printed in Great Britain by
Omnia Books Ltd., Glasgow

Contents

The long rough road

Introduction

Thirty years have passed since 'Too hard For God?' was written, and seventy years since Charles Marsh first set out for the hills of Algeria. The time is right for a fresh generation to know and appreciate this remarkable book and its equally remarkable author.

The time is right because in these turbulent days we see before our eyes the harvest ripening which Charles and Pearl Marsh and others of their generation worked for, longed for, and prayed for. They sowed in tears, walking by faith not by sight, preaching in season and out of season, following those who 'died in faith, not having received what was promised, but having seen it and greeted it from afar.'

How thrilled they would be to meet today's Algerian evangelists, pastors, teachers, writers, broadcasters and translators – leaders of vibrant local churches faithfully continuing the work for which they gave everything! Their daughter Daisy, herself a servant of Christ among Algerians all her life, has agreed to write an additional chapter to her father's book, bringing the story up to date. Her testimony provides a glorious affirmation that there truly is 'nothing too hard for God'.

Robin Daniel

From the Introduction to the First Edition

It was difficult to decide on the form in which the book should be written. So much of it is of heartaches and tears, resolution and courage. To speak of such things among a few intimate friends is one thing – to write of them for a wider circle is another. It was, therefore, decided the book should be written in the third person about Abd alMasih (meaning 'the servant of Christ') and Lalla Jouhra ('Lalla' being a religious term of respect for a woman and 'Jouhra' meaning 'Pearl') by which Charles and his wife are known in Algeria.

The dates of the main events in the book are as follows:

1925	The author leaves England for Algeria via France.
1927	He marries Lalla Jouhra in Algiers and they commence work at Lafayette.
1928	Turned out of Lafayette, they go to The Hammam.
1930	They return to Lafayette and The Hammam becomes an outstation.
1945–6	Meeting hall and outstation at Beni Ourtilane established.
1954	Algerian revolution commences.
1962	Independence from France proclaimed.
1969	Last Bible School and camps referred to.

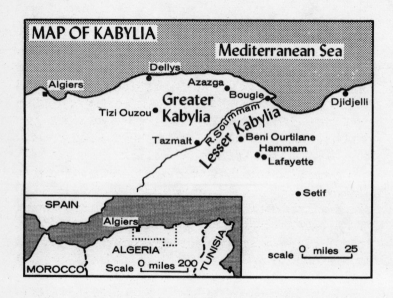

MAP OF KABYLIA

Mediterranean Sea

Algiers

Dellys

Azazga

Bougie

Djidjelli

Greater
Kabylia

Tizi Ouzou

R.Soummam

Lesser Kabylia

Tazmalt

Beni Ourtilane
Hammam
Lafayette

Setif

SPAIN

Algiers

ALGERIA

MOROCCO

Scale 0 miles 200

TUNISIA

scale 0 miles 25

Chapter One

Into Battle

Abd alMasih and Lalla Jouhra walked along the hot dusty road, high in the mountains of Algeria. They had been married just twelve days. The previous night had been spent on the hard damp floor of a room which they had rented from the Kabyles. Why were they there? What were they doing? They were pioneer missionaries. They had come to assault one of the strongholds of Satan, and to win these Muslims of Kabylia for Christ.

At the entrance to the village, custom decreed that they must separate, he to go to the men in the mosque, she to the women in their homes. The heavy oak doors of every house were shut and barred from within. How could this young English bride contact those frightened isolated women, shut away as they were in their harems? She had been brought up in a Kabyle village, and knew well the women's abject fear of strangers, their unwillingness to open the door to anyone whom they did not know. Yet she longed to make contact with them, to be friendly, to sit with them on their mats and talk. A sudden thought struck her. Thirsty and weary as she was from the long walk in the heat of the day, she could ask for a drink. Knocking gently on one door she called,

'*A thamrarth* (Old woman), open the door.' The door was opened a fraction of an inch and the frightened face of a young woman peered out.

'Go away quickly. Clear out. We do not want you,' she said.

'*Sebah alkheyr*' (Good morning), was the friendly greeting.

'Oh, so you are a Kabyle!' said the woman. Her fears were dispelled.

This stranger could speak her language and she spoke it well.

'Who are you? What do you want? Please go away.'

'I am so thirsty. Please give me a drink.'

'Yes, we have a well in our courtyard. Come in and sit down.'

The missionary went into the courtyard; a rush mat was brought, and she sat down. In a few moments she was surrounded by all the women of the house, who touched her hair, stroked her dress, and lifted it up to see what she wore underneath! The bucket was lowered into the well with the long cord plaited from goats' hair, and the pitcher was filled with fresh cold water. Lalla Jouhra shuddered. She knew well that such water might be contaminated, but there was nothing for it. She must drink. She tilted the pitcher in such a way that the water ran into her open mouth without touching the vessel with her lips.

'*Alhamdoullah*' (Praise the Lord), she said when she had drunk.

'*Sahha*' (Health), came from every woman.

'Thank you. May He give you good health,' she replied.

Then she produced her New Testament and read to them a story of the woman at the well. How surprised they were that a woman could read! Never, never in their lives had they heard of such a thing. Only boys and men learned to read. She read on, 'Whosoever drinketh of this water shall thirst again, but whosoever drinketh of the water that I shall give him shall never thirst . . .' The women listened intently, gripped by the message.

Suddenly their faces changed colour, fear and terror seized them. Turning round, Lalla Jouhra understood the reason. Corning towards her was an old hag with a demonic expression on her face. She seemed the very personification of evil. She was the old lady of the house, and ruled her household with a rod of iron. She had suffered in her youth, and was determined to make her daughters-in-law suffer by every means in her power. Now one of them had dared to let this stranger into their courtyard, into her house. She would pay dearly for this; but first she must deal with the stranger. Meanwhile every woman fled.

'What has brought you here? You have come here to tell these stories about your Jesus. May God curse you and your religion,' she howled. Nearer and nearer she drew, until her evil face almost touched the pure face of the girl. Her vile breath was sickening.

'Come into this room and talk,' she said.

The girl went in, and the old hag slammed the door and turned the key in the lock.

'Now I have got you,' she said, 'I will shut you up and force you to marry my son. You will just disappear. Before your husband knows where you are it will be too late. I'll teach you. Take that, and that!' She spat again and again, her vile spittle directed full into the face of the girl. Again she spat and cursed; working herself into a frenzy of rage.

Suddenly the old woman opened the door of the courtyard and with a tremendous effort, thrust the servant of God outside. She fell headlong in the dust and dirt of the narrow lane. She had come to win these women for Christ, 'come with a message of love', only to be met with bitter hatred and scorn.

She rose from the ground, the dust and filth clinging to that awful spittle. Women appeared from nowhere. They

pulled her into a neighbouring courtyard, wiped the filth
from her dress, and offered clean water for her to wash her
face and hands.

'Come into our yard,' they said. 'That old woman is
cruel and wicked. Her daughters-in-law have told us of
your wonderful Book. Read it to us.'

'But how did they get here when they are shut away?'
asked Lalla Jouhra.

'Oh, that is easy. They climbed over the roof and
dropped down into our yard. Look, here come some
more.'

Three more women had climbed into the fig tree and
now dropped to the ground in the courtyard.

'We are all waiting for a new bride to be brought,' they
said. 'Read something to us while we are waiting.'

So the Lord began to open doors.

A week later an experienced missionary accompanied
Abd alMasih while Lalla Jouhra remained at home. The
two men sat on the large stone slabs in front of the mosque
of that fanatical village. Nearly a hundred Kabyles had
gathered, and the older man, who spoke Kabyle well, read
to them from the Psalms, 'Blessed is he whose transgres-
sion is forgiven, whose sin is covered.'

'There is no forgiveness for anyone outside the religion
of Islam,' shouted the *sheikh*, the religious leader of the
village.

'Do you believe in Mohammed?' said another.

'We do not want to hear about Moses and David and
Jesus, but only about Mohammed,' yelled a third with a
scornful smirk on his face.

'*Chehed* (witness), say "There is no god but Allah, and
Mohammed is the Apostle of God." ...' In a moment every
man was on his feet, shouting vociferously:

'Testify, testify, tell us that *you* believe in Mohammed.

May God curse your religion! May He blind you! May He send you to hell fire!'

The malicious curses were hurled at them from every quarter. A hand shot out and struck the younger man's throat. The unexpected blow caused him to stagger backwards. Another man deliberately cleared his throat and spat viciously. The tumult was such that the older man could proceed no further. He had just read one verse of a Psalm, and with this din it was impossible to make himself heard.

The situation was extremely ugly. How could they escape from this angry mob? In fanatical frenzy the Muslims shouted and screamed, moving closer and closer. The old man folded his arms, gazed at them and smiled. If he was perturbed he would not show it.

'Look, he is not afraid. He is laughing at us,' they said.

There was a moment of dead silence, the tension lessened.

'Come along, we must go,' he said to his companion, and the crowd opened up to let him pass.

'Go and may the curse of God rest on you for ever,' the voice of the old Muslim sheikh rang out in a final malediction. He had chased them from his village.

Outside the village, the veteran missionary said to the young pioneer: 'You must never, no never return here alone. It is far too dangerous. You will be killed.' . . . Yet God called him. God had sent him to that village, to these tribes of fanatical men. He **MUST** go back . . . alone.

Thus from the very first days Abd alMasih and Lalla Jouhra realised that they were engaged in a spiritual conflict. They had come with a message of peace and goodwill, only to be met by bitter antagonism and intense hatred. They could say with Paul, 'Our fight is not against any physical enemy: it is against organisations and powers that are spiritual. We are up against the unseen power that controls this dark world, and the spiritual agents from the very headquarters of evil.' Ephesians 6:10 (Phillips).

Could these two inexperienced young people win through in the face of this bitter opposition? He alone with men? She alone with the women? The Lord sent out His disciples two by two, but workers among Muslims must nearly always plough a lone furrow. In the early days of their missionary life Lalla Jouhra accompanied Abd alMasih on his visits to the villages, but a strange man can never enter a Muslim house with his wife. She could never sit with him among the men. Each must go alone. Two lone workers among a population of over a quarter of a million. Could they possibly succeed? Could they win at least some of these Muslims for the Lord?

By the grace of God they did. This book tells how it is possible to reach with the gospel those whom many regard as 'too hard for God!' It tells of God's faithfulness and power, of His many and varied ways of working: ways which are not always our ways. It tells of His victory in Muslim lives, and some methods by which the gospel is spread in Eastern lands.

The lands of Northern Africa have always been regarded as one of the hardest parts of the great world field. The men who inhabit these countries are the descendants of those who destroyed the early Christian churches. They are proudly conscious of this fact. The inhabitants are all Muslims, and Islam is engrained in their very characters, indelibly impressed on their minds. The population can be divided into Berbers and Arabs. The Berbers, of whom the Kabyles are the chief branch, were driven into the mountains by the invading Arabs. Two waves of invasion swept over the land, the first in A.D. 647, followed by that of the tenth century.

The religion of Algeria is Islam, which means, *surrender to God*. A man who follows Islam is called a Muslim or Moslem. He professes to surrender himself wholly to God. Both Kabyles and Arabs are Muslims. They believe that Abraham was the first Muslim, although it is obvious that he did not and could not follow the tenets of their religion, but he did trust God unreservedly and implicitly obeyed His commands.

Kabylia is a mountainous region and almost the entire population lives in the villages. These villages are often built on the crest of the hills, and are accessible only by steep narrow paths.

Kabylia is that part of Algeria that extends along the coast from Dellys to Djidjelli, and inland from the Mediterranean to a depth of fifty miles. It is divided into two regions, Lesser and Greater Kabylia. Lesser Kabylia extends to the east and south of the Soumam river (see map).

Professor Sayce traces the Kabyles to the Amorites of the Old Testament. They are a white-skinned race with European characteristics. Their mountain strongholds were never fully subdued by the Romans. Successive invasions of Arabs, Turks and French failed to assimilate them. They have retained their Berber language with its dialects of Greater and Lesser Kabylia. Missionaries and others have reduced these to writing, but the language varies from tribe to tribe and often from village to village.

The people can be divided into two classes, Kabyles and Marabouts, but all speak Kabyle and are ardent Muslims. The Marabout families claim to be the direct racial descendants of Mohammed, but probably came into the country from Morocco through religious pioneers of Islam. They are the upper class, men and women of character, genteel and polite, even though they may be desperately poor. They live in different villages from the

Kabyles, or in a separate part of the same village. A Marabout may take a Kabyle girl in marriage, but a Marabout girl may not be given to a Kabyle man.

Kabyle men usually wear two garments, an under garment or tunic called a *gandourah*, and a loosely flowing outer garment, woven without a seam, which is called a *burnous*. The red *thachachith* or skull cap denotes them as Muslims. Lesser Kabylia has come more under the influence of Islam and many of the men wear a white turban. Those who work in the towns or who have been to France usually wear European clothes. Kabyle women always wear brightly coloured scarves on their heads and dresses which reach to their ankles. If a young woman or a Marabout girl goes out she usually prefers to wear a long white *alhaf* or shawl which envelops her whole body, and a veil which covers her face, leaving one or both eyes showing. In the towns the younger women are fighting for the abolition of the veil and many go about unveiled and dressed in European clothes. Many of the Kabyles are highly intelligent. They are capable of intense and strong emotions, are deeply affectionate to their friends, but bitterly opposed to their enemies and can become bigoted religious fanatics. A Kabyle is trustworthy and will never betray a friend or one who is under his protection, and for this characteristic the writer owes the Kabyle people a debt of deep gratitude that he can never repay. Rugged mountaineers, they bear the stamp of their environment.

A Kabyle man

A Kabyle woman

Carrying water

Chapter Two

The Call and Preparation

'These people have never heard of our Saviour,' the older missionary said. 'No one has ever been to tell them the wonderful news of salvation.' Deep in the heart of young Abd alMasih the conviction was born, 'I am the man to tell them. This is my corner of the great world field.'

They stood on the narrow stony track nearly five thousand feet up in the mountains of Kabylia. Nearly fifty miles away, the stately snow-capped Atlas mountains raised their heads. Range after range of mountains and foothills extended as far as the eye could see, the villages fringing the hilltops. Abd alMasih and his companion gazed entranced at the magnificent panorama. At their feet was a group of five large villages, each with its mosque into which the men streamed for the Friday prayer. The low monotonous chanting of the boys and students arose as they recited the Koran, and the strident voice of the *muezzin* rang out calling the faithful to prayer. More than fifty villages were visible, and hundreds more lay hidden in the valleys and behind the mountains.

Abd alMasih was to be married in a week's time. Then he and his wife would launch out as pioneers in the mountainous district of Lesser Kabylia. He had gone to Algeria in association with an evangelical Mission and for fifteen months after his arrival, he had applied himself diligently to the study of the Kabyle language, working twelve to fifteen hours a day. Then the Mission had sent him to a town where only Arabic was spoken. His heart sank. Had all those months of diligent study of Kabyle been in vain? Must he start at once to learn yet another language? Could it be God's will for him and his wife to start work in an Arab town, with the nearest Kabyle village fifty miles away?

The whole morning of the preceding day had been spent in a fruitless search for a lodging, or home in the large Arab town. The conviction had grown on him that God had called him to the Kabyles, and now that certainty deepened as he looked out on those villages. A deep compassion, an irresistible yearning gripped his soul.

'We must be getting back,' said his companion, breaking in on Abd alMasih's reverie, 'but on our way we will call at the administrative centre of Lafayette, and see if we can find a house for you to live in. I must warn you that this is extremely unlikely, and the Mission said that you must work in the town of Setif.' Ten minutes after arriving at Lafayette the house was found and secured by the payment of the first month's rent. There was no long search. God opened the door. This was where they were to start. Thus God confirmed to His servant, through the working of His Providence, the inward urge of the Holy Spirit in his heart. During the more than forty years of service that followed, he could never look out over that vast panorama of mountains without being deeply moved, and feeling the continual yearning to reach out to those villages to tell of salvation through faith in Christ.

Several years previously a veteran missionary from Algeria had visited the church which Abd alMasih attended. He had spoken of the Lord's work in Muslim lands and had told of a visit that he had recently paid to a part of

Algeria that was completely unevangelised. In one village, the Muslim men had pleaded with him to settle among them, promising to give him a one-roomed house, rent free, five fig trees, about five pounds a year, a sheep at their annual feast and as many eggs as he could eat!

'The door is wide open to this tribe, the people are without a witness for Christ, and there is no one to go,' said the speaker. 'The Lord Jesus said, "Go ye into all the world and preach the gospel to every creature" and that includes Muslims.'

As he listened to that servant of God telling of this open door, Abd alMasih had felt that inner urge, an urge of the Holy Spirit convincing him that he must go to Algeria. God needed him there. This was God's work, but it was also *his* work. The meeting concluded with the singing of the hymn,

> 'Thy life was given for me!
>   Thy blood, O Lord, was shed
> That I might ransomed be,
>   And quickened from the dead.
> Thy life was given for me:
>   What have I given for Thee?'

During the singing of that hymn he decided to place his life completely under the control of the Lord Jesus. With all his heart Abd alMasih had sung the last verse,

> 'To Thee my all I bring,
>   My Saviour and my King!'

Thus it was that he had heard the call of God.

There had followed long years of waiting, years when his spirit had chafed at the discipline of marking time, but had it not been for those years of testing in the homeland, he and his partner would never have been able to face the long years of arduous service that followed. One thing they knew. They had been called. They must go on.

Many young people long to know just how the call of God will come to them. There must be a complete surrender to the Lord of the whole life, and a willingness to do God's will. God rarely reveals His will to one who merely desires to know it. He always reveals His will to the one who is prepared to follow, at whatever cost. 'Anyone who resolves to do the will of God will know' (John 7:17), is the promise to which Abd alMasih clung. God assured him, 'The meek will He guide in judgement: and the meek will He teach His way.' (Psalm 25:9).

He found that there was a close correspondence between his call to salvation and his call to service. God used three things to bring him to Christ: a passage of Scripture, His servants and the conviction that he must do something about it. He had cast himself unreservedly upon the Lord Jesus Christ for salvation. Then God had called him to His service. Again He had brought certain Scriptures very forcibly to his mind. The call had come through hearing the missionary speak. There had again been that inward compulsion, that conviction that he must act, the realisation that he must do something about it. The Lord Jesus Christ must be trusted implicitly and followed unreservedly. When God calls to His service, He usually speaks by means of a verse or a passage of Scripture, and He also gives that inner conviction, 'I am the man.' 'I am the woman.' 'This is MY work.'

Long years of experience have shown that this is the pattern. Each is called in a special and unique way, but the call usually comes through a human instrument, by the reading of a book, or listening to a missionary report. When this is accompanied by an inward urge and conviction, a young believer would do well to take trusted servants of God into his confidence. There are often obstacles to be overcome, faith is often tested but, in His all-wise providence, God leads on step by step. Looking back over the years one can see that He makes no mistakes.

Abd alMasih and Lalla Jouhra were married in Algiers in the month of May. In order to commence the Lord's work as soon as possible they decided to forego a honeymoon, spending just one day at a seaside resort. Then they took the long train journey to Setif where they spent the night. The next day they left at 5 a.m. on a ramshackle bus to travel to Lafayette. People looked at them with undisguised interest. Neither Europeans nor Arabs had ever seen missionaries before. How strangely alone and inexperienced they felt! The bleak barren mountains of the High Plateaux were in such striking contrast to the beautiful country of Kabylia. They soon discovered that, although Lafayette was the administrative centre of the Kabyle tribes of the Guergour, the language of the people was Arabic. The first Kabyle villages were still twenty miles distant. They had no transport. How could they possibly reach these villages?

A bus left each day between noon and 3 p.m. for Guenzet, returning the next morning. They were able to rent an unfurnished room in a native courtyard, and it was here that they planned to spend two nights each week. The seats of the bus were made to accommodate five persons, but frequently eight were crammed into this limited space. The thick woollen burnouses worn by the men restricted any movement once people were packed in like sardines. The roof was loaded with merchandise of every description. When no more people could be packed into the limited interior of the vehicle, others were told to climb on to the roof. There they sat with their feet over the sides, dangling in the faces of the passengers below! In places the road was so narrow that it was impossible for the bus to negotiate the corners. It would proceed as far as possible, reverse, and then just manage to scrape the cliff face on one side with the motor overhanging the precipice. There were many exciting and hair-raising episodes.

Many were the accidents on these dangerous mountainous roads. Abd alMasih will never forget the truck which had got out of control, overturned and caught fire. Within seconds it was a blazing mass. Ten veiled women had been packed into the back part, together with two sheep and several children. The canvas back and sides had been tightly laced so that no one could see the women. They could not get out and the two men in front made no attempt to save them. They were all burned to death.

God in His mercy protected His servants throughout the years from any serious accident. On this their first trip on one of these ramshackle buses they arrived in the large village of Guenzet just before dark. A motley crowd of men and children met the bus, and there was much speculation as to the identity of the two strangers. They were glad to gain the shelter of the rented room. It measured nine feet square, with a stone cobbled floor, and a thatched roof from which dropped a succession of small insects. There was no window, no fireplace, no light. The floor was reeking with moisture, as it had been used for storing salt. They planned to spend two nights each week in this cold, damp, unfurnished room.

Having unpacked their bags and eaten a cold supper by the light of a candle, they prepared to sleep on the one camp bed that they possessed. It would not accommodate two, so in spite of the state of the floor the sleeping bag was spread on a groundsheet. The moisture soon seeped through both the groundsheet and the bag. There was little sleep that night. The battle was on between these two inexperienced young missionaries and the hosts of darkness.

At 4 a.m. the call of the muezzin rang out over the sleeping village from the large mosque next door to where the young missionaries were lying. Then it was taken up by each of the eight mosques. 'Come to prayer. Prayer is better than sleep.' How near it seemed to Abd alMasih and his young bride! The low drone of voices came over as the men recited their prayer. Now it was time to go to the mosque and make the acquaintance of these fanatical men, to win them from antagonism to allegiance to the King of kings. But first the missionaries themselves bowed in prayer.

'We rest on Thee – our Shield and our Defender!
We go not forth alone against the foe;
Strong in Thy strength, safe in Thy keeping tender,
We rest on Thee, and in Thy Name we go.'

The sun was just rising above the horizon as Abd alMasih left the shelter of that room. 'The Lord be with you, darling. I shall be praying for you,' said Lalla Jouhra. She turned the key in the lock, shutting herself in to commence her lonely vigil. Never had the young man so felt his utter weakness. His heart was filled with misgivings and fear. 'I rest on Thee, and in Thy Name I go.' He reached the mosque. The men had finished their prayer. Some were seated on the stone benches. Others were standing round discussing plans for the day. He sat down.

'*Sebah kum belkheyr*' (Good morning to you all), he said.

'*Merahba bik*' (Welcome), they replied. 'Tell us, are you a good Muslim?'

'Have you prayed the morning prayer?'

'Witness to Mohammed. Say there is no god but God ...'

'Was Jesus the Son of God? or was He just the son of Mary?'

'Tell us, how many prophets are there?'

'Who is the last, the greatest, the seal of the prophets?'

'Did Jesus die or was He taken alive to heaven?'

In rapid succession the questions came and to attempt to answer them was useless. They did not mean that he should.

He produced his New Testament in Kabyle, and read a verse or two to them.

'We do not understand that book. It is not our language. It is not even good Kabyle,' they said.

They did not want to listen. Their voices increased to a loud roar, while his young wife listened from the shelter of that windowless room. She wondered if he would be torn to pieces by the fanatical mob.

She dared not go and join him, but she could pray. How thankful she was to hear his knock, and see his face once again! He joined her for a cup of coffee before they set out to tramp to the surrounding villages.

A discreet cough outside told them that someone had called to see them. It was the young Kabyle man who had rented the room to them. He was immaculately dressed in a European suit, but wore a white turban and black patent shoes. He was obviously a Kabyle gentleman who knew how to behave. He accepted a cup of coffee, and Lalla Jouhra produced the cake which she had made and which was to last them for three days. Cutting a slice of the cake, she offered it to her visitor. 'Thank you so much,' he replied, 'but it is rather a lot,' and, to the consternation of Lalla Jouhra, he took the cake, leaving the slice! This was true etiquette, for the host always breaks off a piece of bread, and eats it to show that the food is not poisoned. Then he hands the remainder to his guest. True politeness, but she knew better next time. That is how one learns!

As soon as their visitor had left them, they set out to walk to the villages. The surrounding landscape was picturesque and delightfully green in the morning sun. Behind them the mountains were covered with a forest of cork oak and Aleppo pine. To their left, in the distance, a series of bare scree-girt ridges were scoured by deep gorges and ravines. The swift-flowing streams of the winter were beginning to dry up. The slope of the mountain below them was terraced to provide small gardens where vines, pomegranates and figs would flourish later in the year. The fields on the lower slopes were divided into minute plots, where barley, lentils, peas and beans were growing. Prickly pears grew everywhere and there were a few orange trees. Nearer the sea, walnuts, oranges, and grapefruit abounded. They were struck by the resemblance to the Biblical description of Canaan in Deuteronomy 8:7–9.

On that first day they visited four villages before returning to their room. They found that the Kabyles were very hospitable and usually welcomed them to their village, but, as soon as they found out the object of their visit, their attitude would often change to suspicion and hostility. Throughout that first summer and autumn they continued these weekly visits, reaching out to the villages within a radius of eight or nine miles and returning to sleep in the cold bleak room. But they had not yet been accepted by the people nor had they won their way into their hearts. The bus left at 5 a.m. on the following day for the return journey, but they had to be at the terminus at least half an hour beforehand in order to get a place. This method was terribly time consuming and tiring and they decided to try and buy a motor cycle and side-car. The Lord had seen their faithful efforts to witness to others, and He had a better plan in store. Without any seeking on their part, a kind donor gave the money to buy a small car, a luxury for many in those days, but an essential if those hundreds of villages were to be reached. How good the Lord is! 'Before they call I will answer.'

Kabylia

The bus on which they travelled

The mosque at Guenzet

Chapter Three

Outreach

The provision of the small car enabled the two pioneers to extend the range of their activities greatly. In an ever-increasing outreach Abd alMasih eventually evangelised over five hundred villages in Lesser Kabylia. The villages are often perched on the mountain crests, and sometimes hidden in the valleys. In places there are as many as six hundred inhabitants to the square mile. Each village is administered by an assembly of elders, and the chief of these is called the *amin*. Local codes of law deal with all questions of property and general offences.

Each village can be traced back to the man who in antiquity was its founder. His sons married and formed the various quarters of the village. Villages are usually divided into *sofs* or rival clans, which were originally matrimonial fractions.

Of the five hundred villages which Abd alMasih reached more or less regularly with the gospel, only twenty-five were situated on any sort of motor road. The rest had to be reached on foot. This meant tramping for four to six hours a day over rough stony roads, fording streams, climbing up to a village four thousand feet up and then down to the valley, before climbing up to the next village. Lalla Jouhra could not accompany him to these outlying places, so he went alone.

The field could be divided into three districts. Some places could be reached in a day. He would then drive out in the car, leave it on the roadside, and in the early morning, often before it was light, slip away for his long walk. At night he would return to the car, to find it intact, untouched, and ready for the long journey home. Only on one occasion during thirty-seven years was it broken into, and then by a stranger to the district. Another set of villages could be reached by spending the night in a distant village, visiting hamlets and villages on the way out and back. This would occupy two days. A third group could be reached only by an extended effort. Loading all that he needed for ten days or more on to the back of a donkey, he would tramp from village to village. Alternatively, he would take a tent and pitch it at convenient points along a motor road, walking down to the villages during the day. A special effort to reach the distant tribes was made every spring and autumn, usually for a period of ten days.

The Kabyles are a community-loving people and, when the day's work is ended, they gather in groups in the mosque, the coffee house or the local *thejmath*. The thejmath is a covered building at the entrance to the village. It is here that the village elders meet. It is often bordered by large flat stones which serve as seats, worn smooth and shiny by ages of use. The Kabyles are most industrious and, during the day, they work in the fields, ploughing, reaping, gathering olives or figs or making olive oil with their primitive olive presses that date from Biblical times.

In the summer, during the heat of the day, twenty or thirty men will gather in the thejmath, and towards sunset as many as a hundred. This is the best place for a gospel meeting and a respectful hearing is often given to the message.

It was four o'clock in the morning on a cold winter's day. Hoar frost covered the ground, there was the nip of snow in the air, and the upper slopes of the surrounding mountains were already deep in snow. Bed was certainly the best place on such a day, reflected Abd alMasih. Yet there were still hundreds of people who had never heard. 'How shall they hear without a preacher?' And he was that preacher. So out of bed, a quick cup of coffee, a bite of bread and a rapid check-up. The previous evening he had packed into his bag some tracts, a Bible, sandwiches for midday, an orange, a handful of figs, dental forceps, a mac and, last but not least, a good selection of literature supplied by the Scripture Gift Mission in French, Kabyle and Arabic. Locking the door he went out into the night.

The morning star shone brightly in the east; the smallest sound echoed in the clear mountain air as he drove his car along the winding road, the frost crackling under the wheels. A sudden turn in the road, and dark forms loomed up in the car lights. He stepped on the brakes only just in time to avoid a herd of twenty camels lumbering along with their clumsy gait, each carrying a quarter of a ton of wheat.

Half an hour later he parked his car just off the road. The first streaks of dawn were visible in the east. Not a soul could be seen as he locked the car, and committed it to the keeping of the One who through the years had never failed. He set out to reach the villages. Arriving at the river, he took off his boots and socks, rolled up his trousers as high as was possible and stepped into the icy water. It swirled by swiftly, swollen by the melting snow. Tears came into his eyes. It was terribly cold. Large stones, rolled along by the stream, battered his ankles and legs. His feet were almost carried from under him, but he forged on. Suddenly he stumbled into a hole in midstream, the water up to his hips. 'What a fool you are, go back,' said an inner voice. 'Go ye,' said his Lord. He must go on, so hurling his boots across the river he pushed on step by step. There was no going back now. Wet and cold he finally reached the further bank. Wringing the water from his sodden clothes he put on his socks and boots, and set off on foot for the long six-mile walk.

The sun rose above the hills as he toiled up the last long climb to the village. He found the men sitting round the small square and greeted them.

'Good morning to you all,' he said.

'May God give you a good morning,' they replied. 'Where have you come from? Where did you spend the night?'

'In my home,' he answered.

'Impossible.'

'Well, I did.'

'Then who carried you over the river? You have no animal.'

'I forded the river as you do. I came over on my feet.'

'But why, so early in the morning?'

'I think you all know why. I have a message for you from the Word of God. Will you stay and listen?' And they did.

The men quickly brought a large mat which they spread on the ground so that he could sit down. Taking off his boots, he sat cross-legged on the mat, and waited for the men to gather round. Some still stood at a distance, so he produced from his bag a large picture of the Brazen Serpent which he had mounted on calico. Unfolding the picture he spread it on the mat, opened his Bible and let them examine the painting, ask questions and comment. Then, when a sizeable group had gathered, he started to read the Scriptures.

The meeting over, one man said, 'Come along to my house, and share my breakfast. At this time of the year we eat before we go to work.' They went into a closed-in yard and the man called to his wife, 'Smail, bring the mat.' A man will never call his wife by name or speak of her. He uses the name of his eldest son to call her. The woman came out carrying the mat, meanwhile turning away her face, returning shortly afterwards with a basket on which was a hot loaf of bread and some figs. The bread had been made into cakes about fifteen inches in diameter and half an inch thick. The woman had baked these on a griddle over the wood fire. The art of cooking is to turn the bread at the appropriate moment, so that both sides are cooked. This was cooked to perfection. The man broke the bread into pieces, ate a piece himself and passed the rest to Abd alMasih. Breaking off a small piece he dipped it into the bowl of olive oil and munched it with a fig. It was a wholesome breakfast to which he did justice. The woman called the man, who went away and returned bringing a dish of olive oil in which floated four eggs. Said he, 'You need strength to walk over our mountains'.

Then he took him to see a poor suffering lad who had not left the dark room in which he lay for many months. He was a bag of bones, covered with bed sores and the stench was abominable. No doctor ever visited that village, so Abd alMasih cared for the lad as best he could before he left for the next village.

He soon discovered that sharing in some measure their lives, facing their hardships, eating their food, caring for their sick, sitting where they sat, listening, sympathising, was the way to Kabyle hearts. This was our Lord's way. This was Paul's way. Thus over the years Abd alMasih gradually saw the attitude of these rough mountaineers change from hostility to friendliness and trust.

When he left that village the men were already setting out to work. Driving a couple of oxen before them, carrying the heavy plough on their shoulders, they walked from two to five miles each day to their fields. The next village was three miles away. There Abd alMasih found a smaller group of men surrounding blind Hamid.

Hamid was expounding to them the doctrines of the Koran, emphasising his words with a stick which he held stretched before him. Afflicted by blindness from his birth, unable to work, he had spent many years in a Koranic school, listening to others repeating the lines of the sacred book, until he had learned to recite it by heart. He knew all the favourite arguments of the local sheikhs, and the fundamental doctrines of Islam. Abd alMasih seated himself with the men. The blind man stopped speaking and for a few minutes listened attentively to the gospel message. Then he opened fire with a volley of questions. He did not wait for a reply to any of these questions. He did not want an answer. His aim was to show how much he, a blind man, knew of his religion. At any price he must stop these other men from hearing the gospel. Abd alMasih sought to reply to Hamid's questions, but as the latter became more and more excited and the meeting was degenerating into a useless discussion, he decided to play his trump card.

'Tell us what Mohammed has really done for you, my friend. I will give you ten minutes to tell us and during that time I will remain silent. Then you will listen for ten minutes as I tell you what Christ has done for me.' The bargain was struck.

'You speak first,' said Abd alMasih. Hamid began, 'Mohammed has told us to bear witness to him, to pray five times a day, to fast, to give alms, to read the Koran ... That is what he did for us Muslims.'

'Go on,' pleaded the servant of God, 'Tell us what he has *done* for you.'

A minute had passed but he needed no more time.

Mohammed had told him to do so much. He knew it all by heart, but . . . Then very simply Abd alMasih told from a full heart all that Christ had done for him. 'The Lord Jesus has saved me, He has transformed my life. He is my constant friend and companion, giving me strength to follow God and the assurance of forgiveness. He has taught me to love my enemies. He is soon coming back, not to reign for forty years, but to reign for ever. He is coming to take me to be with Him for ever.' Poor blind Hamid could contain himself no longer. He cursed and spat at Abd alMasih, who felt it was useless to continue.

Walking down the village street he could still see the upturned face, the gesticulating stick, the vehement way in which Hamid spat as he cursed him. Oh, the infinite pathos of those poor sightless eyes, as that ignorant Muslim tried to teach his fellows, a blind leader of the blind! He made his way to the next village, reflecting on the seeming paradox that this bitter opposition in one village is often counteracted by heart hunger in the next. Yet how true to the pattern in the Acts of the Apostles!

An hour's walk brought him to the entrance of the next village. Piles of black olives were spread out in the sun. A middle-aged man was buying them, weighing them on a large weighing machine.

'Where are you going, sheikh?' he said.

'I am going to the coffee house to speak to the men about God.'

'Well, just sit down and tell me here.'

'No, I am going to where I can find the men.'

'O.K. then. I will come too, for last week my son was in your meeting and he told us all that he heard. We believe in Jesus, but we do not understand His work. We want to know.' He left his work to come and listen.

The coffee house was crowded with men. Some were playing dominoes, some gambling with cards, some merely sipping cups of black coffee. Abd alMasih removed his shoes at the entrance, walked across the mats and sat down. He ordered a cup of coffee and watched it being prepared. A small charcoal fire was burning in the angle made by two walls. Over this fire a tin of water was boiling. The proprietor put several spoonfuls of coffee powder into a small coffee pot, and added as many spoonfuls of sugar. The coffee had been pounded to a fine powder with a pestle made from the axle of a lorry in a mortar hewed from solid stone by the Romans centuries before! The coffee pot was a small tin can soldered on to a short handle about one foot long. Each customer's coffee was made in a separate pot, and seven or eight of these were placed round the fire. The coffee was brought to the boil, and as it rose in the pot it was tapped lightly. This was done three times. The extreme cold had passed, or the man would have added cayenne pepper to give an added zest. The proprietor poured the thick syrupy mixture into a small tin pot with a tiny lid, placed it beside a cup and handed it to Abd alMasih. He sipped it for a while, making as much noise with his mouth as was possible in order to show his appreciation of the good coffee! Then he appealed to the men to leave their games for just ten minutes while he read to them from the Bible.

He had to condense the message, so he read 1 Timothy 1:15. He was most impressed by the attitude of one man who listened intently. There was a moment's distraction outside. In a minute the coffee shop emptied. The interested man remained. Drawing near he whispered,

'Tell me just what I am to believe.' Abd alMasih read to him from Isaiah 53:6.

'Ah, I see now. My sins on Him. He carried them. He paid. Thank you.'

The men returned and once more he was a Muslim among Muslims. Abd alMasih finished his message and prepared to leave. Once more the man spoke up, 'Tell me, sheikh, are there any who believe in the Lord Jesus in this land, any Kabyles?' Oh, the dread of being alone!

Abd alMasih walked on for half an hour to the next village and went at once to the small mosque in the middle of the village, for he usually found the men sitting on the flagstones which paved the yard in front of it. No men were to be seen, but the drone of voices came from the interior. A lad informed him that a new Muslim sheikh had been installed and that he had called the whole male population to come and learn the Koran. It was quite obvious to Abd alMasih that he was not wanted, so rather sadly he shouldered his bag and walked away. He had not gone more than ten paces when a man called to him from the mosque.

'O sheikh, are you going away without reading to us? Have you no message at all for us from the Word of God?'

'Oh, you have engaged a new sheikh who is teaching you the Koran, and you certainly do not want me,' he said.

'Come back to us. Come into the mosque and read to us,' was the reply. This invitation was too good to be refused. He removed his boots at the entrance to the mosque, placed them with those of the men, and went in to be introduced to the new sheikh. The men said to the new sheikh,

'Put away your books, this man came and taught us when we had no one. We are going to listen to him.' To Abd alMasih they said,

'We are waiting. Read.'

The new Koranic sheikh listened for about ten minutes, and then rose and left without a word. The other men remained for half an hour and greatly appreciated the gospel message.

Abd alMasih visited just one more village before starting the long walk back to his car. Fording the river, he found the car in good condition, and had soon covered the half-hour's run home. He had been away fourteen hours.

Chapter Four

Learning The Language

'Abd alMasih, how long did it take you to learn the language?' said the young worker.

'Which language do you mean?' he replied, and added, 'I am still learning them all.'

Arriving in Algeria, the first three months he had spent in rubbing up his schoolboy French, then he started to study Kabyle. He could not wait to go through the grammar with his teacher – one lesson at a time – but read it through as a text book from beginning to end! He would read on and on until his head nearly split and then put it aside. In this way he obtained a general grasp of the grammar at the same time as he worked systematically through it. He also started to study the Kabyle New Testament. A list of thirty new words was written out each day to be learned by heart. A list was hung by his mirror when shaving, carried in his hand when walking and, on the rare occasions when he saw his fiancée, he was reputed to have courted her with the list of words in one hand and the other arm round her! Learning a language was never easy for him. He had to reduce each word to writing, to see it first in order to learn it and retain it. He set himself the task of learning by heart the lexicon attached to Boulifa's Second Year Grammar. He found that this served him in good stead in after years. Then he tackled grammars written by Hanoteau, and Ben Sedira.

Ten weeks after starting this difficult language he was invited to tour the villages for ten days with his future father-in-law. He shared a mule with another young missionary and, as he rode or walked, he carried on a conversation with the Kabyle muleteer. Making a selection of appropriate texts on the Wordless Book, he learned them by heart, asking the muleteer to correct his faulty pronunciation. He added a few words of explanation on each verse, and asked the Kabyle to correct these. Thus ten weeks after starting to study Kabyle, he gave his first message in that language. It was very halting and faulty, but he held the attention of those rough mountaineers for five minutes. In later years he always encouraged the hundreds of language pupils who passed through his hands to start to use the little they knew as soon as possible.

Fourteen months after commencing the study of Kabyle, he passed the first and second year examinations, and was asked by the Mission to open up pioneer work in a new area. The way was now open for marriage. Five long years had passed since their engagement, but they did not regret the decision. The waiting time was long, but they were now both able to start working together and the Lord conferred on them the inestimable privilege of taking the gospel for the first time to those who had never before heard.

At the end of the first year he had certainly learned enough Kabyle to pass his language tests, he could give a direct message and, to some extent, hold an audience, but he found that he did not understand many things that were said to him by others. This is essential in the quick repartee which is so useful in evangelising Muslims, especially in the villages.

He soon found that there are three stages in learning a language. The first is attained when one can speak on everyday subjects and give a message in the language. The second stage is reached when one can understand whatever the other man says, and is able to carry on a conversation on any subject. The last stage is when one can understand all that two nationals are saying when conversing together, follow their idiom, catch their colloquialisms and understand their proverbs. Abd alMasih made this his goal. He quickly realised that one cannot reach a man's heart until one speaks his mother tongue. He found that many of his colleagues had the impression that they could use French, and that it was a waste of time to learn the native idiom. It was a continual sorrow to him to see that such workers seldom stayed for long on the field. They were limited in their outreach, and were often obliged to confine their efforts to students in towns. They never grasped the mentality of the people and were, often quite unconsciously, involved in countless blunders.

He will always thank God that his senior workers arranged to set him free from other responsibilities for the first eighteen months of his missionary life, in order that he might devote himself to language study. He was privileged to be able to listen to such veteran workers as the late Messrs. H. G. Lamb, J. Griffiths and S. Arthur, and as he listened he noted. Never was he found without a notebook and pencil. Every unknown word, useful phrases containing a known word, idioms and proverbs were all assiduously noted and checked with the senior worker. His fiancée also was a tremendous help.

He had reading lessons with one sheikh for three weeks. The chief impression made on him was a series of blains half an inch in circumference covering the whole of his body. He could not escape doing the whole prescribed hour, but as the lessons were given in a room which had been recently vacated by sick folk, and an army of fleas was always crawling over his body, it was almost impossible for him to concentrate. He escaped to the bathroom after one such trial, turned his trousers inside out over a bowl of water, and caught thirty of his tormentors!

Now that Abd alMasih had started as a pioneer he was faced with a series of problems. The Berber language spoken in Lesser Kabylia was a totally different dialect. He eventually found that in reading the New Testament he must change one word in five. He now had no language teacher. The Berber dialect was no longer the major language of the region which was Arabic. A number of people helped him as the years went by. Not least was the young missionary who was determined to start from scratch, unhindered by the mistakes of his predecessors. Putting on one side all dictionaries and grammars, he set to work to translate the story of the Prodigal Son, learning it by heart and rattling it off like a machine gun. He worked in this way for five years and failed to learn the language, but bravely admitted that his failure was due to the fact that he had despised the work of others. It was a lesson Abd alMasih never forgot. He worked through every Kabyle grammar, dictionary and translation, including those made by Roman Catholics. As he read the Scriptures in his home, or in the villages, he observed very closely the facial expressions of the audience. The flicker of a smile or a puzzled look, meant that something was wrong, the thought had been badly expressed. He would note it, and by dint of persevering effort would discover the mistake and rectify it.

He found that nationals were most helpful, but only to a limited extent. They corrected faulty pronunciation once, twice or even three times, but if he did not consistently change his speech, they would adapt themselves and pronounce the word, or frame the sentence, in the same way as he did, repeating his faulty syntax, That was how the jargon of the mission station was produced and perpetuated – those in immediate contact with the missionary could follow his words but, as soon as he endeavoured to make fresh contacts, he was lost. So Abd alMasih resolved to listen to the people to an ever-increasing extent, noting their conversation in coffee houses, in their homes, on the street. As he extended his activities, he added to his vocabulary, and little by little found that his ability to communicate the message increased.

When in later years the Assistant Secretary of the British and Foreign Bible Society asked him how he had discovered the mistakes in the Kabyle New Testament, he was able to reply, 'I found them, Sir, by hard experience, by sitting among the people, and hearing them say continually, "You say this, but your Book says that." ' The need for the suggested revision was immediately agreed.

Thus, little by little, Abd alMasih mastered the difficult Berber dialect of Lesser Kabylia, until after twenty-five years of listening and noting he was able to translate the four Gospels.

A little later, when Abd alMasih and Lalla Jouhra were obliged to live in an Arab village, a knowledge of Arabic became imperative. This is where he ran into real difficulties, for it was his fourth language in as many years. There was no missionary to whom he could turn for help. There was no opportunity of listening to a spiritual message in Arabic. He could turn to no one for help with the religious phraseology and vocabulary.

Si Bedderdin was a young Koranic teacher who knew Kabyle as well as his native tongue. From him Abd alMasih obtained the equivalent of such phrases as 'What is your name?' 'What is this?' 'How much does this cost?' He could then move among the people and gradually add to his vocabulary. From the first days he could go to the market and talk, as well as listen. He soon found that some of the Kabyle words were derived from Arabic, but there was a slight difference in the way they were pronounced. Kabyle is quite a distinct language from Arabic, but it has borrowed much of the religious vocabulary. For two years after starting to speak Arabic he would write out in full every message and learn it by heart.

Gradually he learned to think in both languages. He certainly had the use of grammars and dictionaries, but found that he learned most by conversing with the people and listening to them. He never had a teacher in Arabic. In later years language schools were organised in Algeria, one of which was attended by missionaries from the whole of North Africa. He was chosen by missionaries of Algeria to be responsible for all the Arabic courses both at Chrea and Cap Matifou. The following year he ran a language school where he was teaching Arabic each morning and Kabyle in the afternoons. The boy who was bottom of the form in French found that to be 'in Christ' is to become a new creature. The power of the Holy Spirit enables a man to overcome the barriers of a sluggish mind, an interrupted education, and to do all for the glory of God. But it means hard work.

Abd alMasih found that the biggest snag for the new missionary was the jargon of the mission station, and the mispronunciation of older workers who had, perhaps, arrived in the country late in life. He had to be for ever on the watch for words which were mispronounced. One lady would persist in telling everyone that she was divorced. Since she was a single lady, this caused considerable amusement and some perplexity to those who did not understand that she was trying to say, 'I want this.' She had used a rolled 'r' instead of the 'r' *grasseyé*. He was very guarded in his use of dictionaries, and learned to be suspicious of religious words taken from the vocabulary of the Muslims. He found that the translator of the Kabyle New Testament had looked up the meaning of the word 'wise' in a French-Kabyle dictionary. *Sage* can mean 'wise', or 'well behaved', according to its connotation. There is all the difference in the world between *une sage femme* (a midwife) and *une femme sage* (a wise woman). When mother says to her child, '*Sois sage,*' she means to say, 'Behave yourself.' The translator had chosen the wrong Kabyle word; and one therefore read of 'the five well-behaved virgins' and 'Christ who is made unto us good behaviour!' How could he spot the error? By making a note of the smirk on people's faces when the word was misused, and then finding out where the mistake lay.

Islam is a religion of works, and it is all important to make clear that salvation is by grace and not of works. But good works have a place in every Christian's life. The first translator had chosen the word *alhasanath* for good works. This is quite correct until one remembers that alhasanath are the five good works of the Muslim religion. They are (i) the witness to Mohammed, (ii) the observance of the fast of Ramadhan, (iii) Muslim prayers, (iv) the giving of alms and (v) the pilgrimage to Mecca. The Kabyle proverb maintains that, 'Good works take away sins'. The Kabyle New Testament stated, 'To those who by patient continuance in these five "good works" seek immortality, God grants eternal life.' (Romans 2:7). No Christian believed this, but the Kabyle New Testament stated it. This opened Abd alMasih's eyes and ears. He found many more serious mistakes, and sought to correct them.

Sometimes he made a discovery when visiting another mission station. One young lady missionary told her neighbours that they simply must have a new dog to get to heaven. She meant to say, of course, a new heart. The word for heart is *qelb* and the word for dog is *kelb*. Another said,

'Do you not know us? We are your frogs.' She had wanted to say, 'We are your neighbours,' but she had used a short vowel instead of a long one, and had said, '*jiran*,' instead of '*jeeran*'.

Another, who wished to speed her departing visitor, would say, '*Fee saa. Fee saa*,' but one uses this word only to send off a dog! Fortunately her pronunciation was such that some doubt was left in the Muslim's mind for she said, '*Fiser. Fiser.*'

Abd alMasih found these incidents rather amusing but, to his cost, he found that the mispronunciation of a single letter can have serious consequences. A fellow-missionary who had accompanied him to a distant village where they were to spend the night, admiring a beautiful hunting dog, said to its owner, '*Aqjoun agi inek?*' He had intended to say, 'Is this your dog?' but he had used a hard 'k' instead of a soft one, and had actually made an obscene remark about the dog. Within three minutes the thirty men who composed his audience had disappeared. They were disgusted. It was impossible to give a message. Their attitude developed into open hostility. Abd alMasih and his friend dared not spend the night in that village, and were compelled to leave after sunset to travel through the night to the next hamlet, a thing which is just not done. But it would have been quite impossible, even dangerous, to have stayed on. Once outside the village, Abd alMasih took a man aside and insisted that he should be told what was wrong. 'It is not you,' he was told, 'It is him. He has a filthy tongue.' The poor young missionary was quite innocent, but no amount of explanation or apology would avail. They left in disgrace. He had mispronounced one letter.

The biggest difficulty was the ambiguity of some words because of the difference in dialect. They bear one meaning in Greater Kabylia and an entirely different meaning in Lesser Kabylia. A few examples will suffice, but the words run into hundreds. *Thakherit* can mean a purse in some places, but it is a disgusting word in other parts. *Acheboub* can mean a lady's hair, or that of a certain part of the body. The Kabyles run off the water from the fountain and collect it in water troughs for watering their gardens. These troughs are about three feet deep and eight feet square, and each is called *asaridj*. But the same word the other side of the country means a lake. This was the word used for the lake of Gennesaret. The picture of harassed disciples in a boat floating on a few square feet of water, in peril of their lives, and crying, 'Lord, save us, we perish,' was amusing in the extreme. It took time to discover these differences in meaning and he diligently noted them. The right words had to be found.

Thus by diligent study Abd alMasih sought to perfect his knowledge of the several languages; his aim being, not merely to speak correctly, but to communicate the message. In learning the language, he came to understand the people and with the understanding came a deep love for them and the ability to touch their hearts in some measure with the Word of life.

Chapter Five

The Adversary

In warfare it is of the utmost importance to understand the strategy of the enemy, his potential weapons and his methods of attack. This applies to the spiritual conflict in which Christians are engaged. From the time that the enemy of souls held out to Eve the tempting bait, 'Ye shall be as gods', until the present era, when he is intent on sowing darnel among the wheat, one of his principal activities has been that of imitation. His avowed intention is to be 'like the Most High.' In the religion of Islam we have Satan's masterpiece. It is pervaded with truths from the Bible, yet they are all subtly perverted. The Muslim believes, he bears witness to his faith, he prays, he fasts and he gives alms. All this was true of the early Christians who believed and bore testimony to their faith. They fasted, prayed and gave alms. They regarded themselves as pilgrims in the world and as belonging to a vast brotherhood of believers. All these have been copied by Islam.

This false religion satisfies man's desire for a religion which he can follow, but which allows him full scope for the satisfaction of his lusts. This great antithesis must always exist between Islam and Christianity. Islam is a religion of works. The gospel is by faith. Islam consists of what man does for God: the gospel, of what God does for man.

As Abd alMasih moved among the people he learned more of their religion, and found to an increasing extent that it was inspired by the god of this world. It is still the nearest imitation to Christianity that exists in the world. Muslims trace their descent from Abraham who, they claim, was the first Muslim. They are, they proudly claim, the direct descendants of Ishmael. Christians are the children of Abraham, but as Isaac was, they are the children of promise. Although Abd alMasih had studied Islam theoretically through text books, he now saw it applied to the lives of the people. The text books had taught him that Islam consists of faith and practice. The articles of the Muslim faith are belief in one God, in Angels, in Evil Spirits, in the Day of Judgement, in Heaven and Hell and in the Revealed Books (of which there are four great ones, the Law, the Psalms, the Gospel and the Koran) and in 124,000 Prophets and Apostles, of whom Mohammed is the greatest and last. They have a very fixed doctrine of predestination and believe that the fate of every man is written by God on his forehead, and the will of Allah determines every act of man as well as his final destiny.

On the practical side Islam is founded on five pillars, or bases. These are (i) the witness to Mohammed, (ii) the fast of Ramadhan, (iii) ritualistic prayer, (iv) the giving of alms and (v) the pilgrimage to Mecca. In the next few pages each of these will be shown against the background of personal experience.

(i) The Witness to Mohammed

'Say, "There is no god but Allah, and Mohammed is the Apostle of God," and all will be well, or else . . .'

Abd alMasih was once more out in the villages, high in the mountains and many miles from home. He had loaded all that he needed for ten days on to a diminutive donkey and, taking a Kabyle with him, had set off on foot to reach the forty or fifty villages of three distant tribes. Thirilt is a village on the top of a hill four thousand feet above sea level. He decided to let the Kabyle man go on with the loaded donkey to the crest over which the road passed, while he climbed up to the village. The meeting over, he made his way over the narrow stony track to the rendezvous, but the man was nowhere to be seen. He called, shouted and whistled, but all to no avail. The sun had long since fallen below the horizon, the cold night crept on, and here he was alone, surrounded by tombs, far from home, in an unknown country, carrying only his Bible, some dental forceps and money.

Making his way to the nearest village he found the men at prayer in the mosque. It was the last prayer of the day, one hour after sunset. He explained to them his predicament, and asked for shelter for the night. Their prayers over, a man approached him in the darkness, touched him on the shoulder and said, 'Follow me.' Together they walked along the dark narrow lane with houses on each side. He could just discern the dusky forms of two men clad in their long woollen burnouses. The cold was intense. Suddenly he felt his arms gripped and drawn round behind him, while something hard was pushed into the small of his back. He knew it to be a sharp knife, the instrument that is used so expertly to kill a sheep, to shave a boy's head, or to murder a man. A voice in the darkness said, 'You are completely lost in our mountains, no one knows where you are. You are more than sixty miles from any help and entirely in our hands. You have only to witness to Mohammed to save your life. Just repeat the words, "There is no God but Allah, and Mohammed is the Apostle of Allah" and all will be well, or else . . .' and that hard thing was pushed into his back. Abd alMasih

thought hard. He was at the mercy of these fanatical men.
Life was precious. He had a wife and two children at
home. He shuddered in the dark. This was a real challenge
to his faith. Quietly he replied, 'You must know that I am a
Christian, and that for me to repeat your creed would be to
deny my Lord. In any case, God looks on the heart, and
even if I repeated the words you know that I do not believe
them.' They relaxed their grip, allowed him to proceed
and said, 'Well, we thought we would try and make you a
Muslim.'

He followed them on to their house, ate the warmed-up
remains of a meal they provided and stretched himself on
the mat. Then they left him alone. He rolled himself in the
thick, warm, woollen blankets, spread his handkerchief on
the pillow and went to sleep. Kabyle blankets often swarm
with life, and he did not anticipate passing a good night. But
he was utterly spent after a long tiring day and slept
soundly until morning. When he awoke the sun had risen,
tingeing the mountain tops with shades of red and purple.
The man with the donkey had heard where he was and had
come on from the other village. The new day began.

Tramping on to the next village Abd alMasih reflected
on the keenness of these Muslim men to make a convert to
their faith. They had been fully aware that he was in their
power and they took full advantage of the situation – not
to steal his money or dental forceps – but to endeavour to
make him believe what they believed. He challenged his
own heart, 'Am I just as eager to win men to my Lord?
When I am alone with a Muslim, do I always seek to direct
the conversation to the Person of the Lord Jesus?'

A few weeks later, under completely different circumstances, he was again impressed by an old Muslim's deep
conviction that Muslims alone knew the truth about God
and, for this reason, must share it.

The old man in question was desperately poor and clad only in one filthy flimsy garment. His whole leg had been covered in a mass of ulcers. The stench was abominable but, after weeks of treatment, the sores had healed, and for the last time Abd alMasih applied a dry dressing. There would be no need for the patient to return for further treatment. His gratitude was most touching. Lifting his head and looking into the face of the missionary he said, 'How can I thank you enough? What can I give you? I am so poor, I have nothing to give. Nothing to offer you, but' . . . and a bright smile broke over his face, 'If you will only say, "*La illah ila Allah*," and witness to Mohammed you will go to heaven. Just repeat the words, sheikh, and be saved.' It was the only way in which he could show his gratitude. He pointed to his prophet, a dead prophet who can never save. Again Abd alMasih searched his heart. Was he just as keen as this man?

Every Muslim is thus a witness to his faith. The creed is simple, easily learned and repeated, and the repetition of the formula does not necessarily involve any change in the moral life of the person who repeats it. To repeat the phrase with conviction is to become a member of the vast Muslim fraternity, with the hope of ultimately attaining Paradise.

In the creed the Muslim affirms his belief in the one true God. He is unique, supreme, the only God. His will determines everything. The Muslim is a 'surrendered' man, surrendered to the will of God. The fate of every man is written by God on his forehead and that determines his final destiny, whether of weal or woe. It is useless for man to struggle against what God has decreed. He is the supreme Master, the Judge who at the last day will take all Muslims to heaven, and pitchfork all unbelievers into the blazing fires of hell.

Abd alMasih quickly found that although the Kabyles did not speak Arabic, they were convinced Muslims. Some had learned to repeat the Koran but few understood it. They were ignorant, but bigoted, convinced and fanatical, even more so than their Arab counterparts.

(ii) The Fast of Ramadhan

In common with all missionaries to the Muslims Abd alMasih and Lalla Jouhra quickly discovered that this is the biggest hindrance to the work of God in a Muslim land. They reached the inevitable conclusion that behind this Fast is the maleficent power of the Evil One whose aim from the beginning was to imitate God. If the repetition of the creed is so simple that a child can learn it, the observance of the Fast, which is incumbent on every Muslim, makes very severe demands on the constitution. It also affects the work of God in every way. The Muslim is acutely reminded each year that his salvation is based on works, and not on faith. Since so few Christians have any adequate conception of this Fast, and some even speak of it as the 'Feast' of Ramadhan, it is worth taking a few pages to describe it and its effect on the work.

The observance of this Fast is an obligatory duty for all Muslims. During the month of Ramadhan no food or drink may be taken from early morning until sunset. The beginning of each day's abstinence is theoretically marked by the moment when it is possible to distinguish a white thread from a black one. When in doubt the pious Muslim attempts to thread a needle, but in practice most Muslims have their last meal about 1 a.m. and then go to bed. From then until sunset nothing at all is to be swallowed, the use of snuff and tobacco is forbidden, and no contact may be made with those of the opposite sex. The richer people usually spend their days in sleeping, and the nights of the Fast in feasting and revelry. For the poor, and those who cannot sleep during the day, the long period of sixteen hours without food or drink, in lands where the shade temperature ranges from 90° to 120° Fahrenheit, can be trying in the extreme. It is pitiable to see a fasting Muslim turn his eyes from the refreshing water as he passes the fountain on a hot summer day.

Muslim teachers say that Ramadhan teaches man to master his lusts and dominate his passions, which are strongest when he eats and drinks, for it is then that the devil tempts him. To indulge in such sins as swearing, perjury, lying, calumny and anger is equivalent to breaking the Fast. Yet, long hours without food or drink, coupled with broken sleep, often make people irritable. Men who are used to drinking strong coffee continually, to smoking tobacco and hashish, feel the enforced deprivation of these things, especially during the first days of the Fast. Many Muslim men admit that they are morally worse at the end of Ramadhan than they were at the beginning. It is a recognised thing that the police are always busier during this month than at any other period of the year. Kabyle women are fearful during Ramadhan, for it is then that most divorces take place. Abd alMasih and Lalla Jouhra found that to live in daily contact with the people during this month was like living over a time bomb which might explode at any moment! But for the devout Muslim to fast during this month is to merit a place in heaven, and any Muslim who dies during Ramadhan is assured that he will immediately enter Paradise.

During the Fast a fanatical spirit prevails and, at such a time, the message of the free grace of God strikes like steel into the Muslim's heart. To be told, even by implication, that all his sufferings to obtain salvation are in vain, is like telling a rich Englishman that all the reserves held in the

Bank of England are so much false money and valueless. Ramadhan is one of the chief stays of this religion of good works. To break the Fast for Christ's sake is to incur immediately the wrath of the Muslim community. Those who are not Christians may privately break it with impunity, but the Christian is made to suffer. When challenged he cannot deny that he has eaten. He must be honest. For this reason, many Christians who love the Lord very sincerely, continue to observe this Fast. Until a convert has broken the Fast it is scarcely possible for him to be baptised. In the eyes of all he is still a Muslim. He is still following a religion of works. Paul would have said, 'He is Ishmael and not Isaac.'

So then this month of Ramadhan is a real testing time for all true Christians. They are sorely tempted to follow the crowd in order to escape ostracism and persecution. Some may be tempted to eat secretly while publicly maintaining an attitude of fasting, but such falsehood is dishonouring to the Lord, soul-deadening and self-condemnatory.

Sadeya was a Kabyle woman who dearly loved the Lord Jesus. She had a deep heart yearning to be well pleasing to Him, and as Ramadhan came round each year, she ate and drank, much to the annoyance of the Muslim neighbours. They often taunted her, 'You know very well that it is hard to go without food and drink all day. Fasting is much too hard for you Christians, so you choose the easy way, just like the heathen and you eat like the animals.' Sadeya was much perturbed by these harsh words and waited on the Lord. She discovered in the New Testament that the early Christians did fast, and that for them fasting and prayer were closely linked. She decided that she would fast for one day every month of the year, and spend the day in believing prayer for the salvation of her unbelieving neighbours. She prepared meals for the day for her three children and her husband. Then from six in the morning she gave herself to her lonely vigil in prayer.

The day seemed so long. At midday she was really discouraged. There was no one to share her vigil, and she had exhausted her list of subjects for prayer. Suddenly there was a movement at the door. Her neighbour Zakeea had called in.

'What? You are not doing any work today? You have not even prepared the bread for your husband and children? Must they go hungry all day?'

Sadeya replied.

'No, I am fasting today in order to spend time in prayer.'

'But it is not the month of Ramadhan. Why should you fast now?'

'I cannot fast as you do during Ramadhan, for you fast to merit a place in Heaven. I know that my Lord Jesus died to bring me forgiveness. For me to fast during Ramadhan would be to renounce Him. But I am not afraid to fast, and to deprive myself of food. So I am fasting as did the early Christians. Fasting to pray.'

This made Zakeea really think hard. She left to tell others, while Sadeya spent a long time praying for her. Soon another neighbour came in, and yet another, until five had called, and to each one she was able to explain why she did not need to fast during Ramadhan. Satan had tried to use the Fast to scare her into disobedience, but God graciously overruled, enlightened her from the Word, and Sadeya remained faithful to her Lord.

In the Christian camps for Young People it became increasingly evident that the observance or non-observance of the Fast of Ramadhan is one of the biggest problems that the young convert has to face. The Christian worker is often asked, 'Is it wrong for a Christian to observe the Fast when he knows that he is saved by grace?'

'If our parents compel us to fast when we are Christians, what should we do, obey our parents or God?'

'At boarding school we cannot get food during the day time, and we are compelled to eat with Muslims at night. What should we do? How can we obey the Lord?' Questions such as these are thought provoking. Abd alMasih would reply in some such terms:

'You are well aware that every religious observance in Islam must be preceded by the formulation of intention (*niya*). For instance, the Muslim says, "I intend to pray the noonday prayers," or, "I intend to fast today." Without this "intention" the mere observance of the Fast is invalid. Merely to abstain from food and drink is not sufficient to acquire merit. The intention preceding each day's fast makes it valid. A young Christian should therefore explain to his parents that he believes in the Lord Jesus, and is saved by the grace of God. The aim of Ramadhan is to do something for God and it is part of a religion of works. He will continue in these terms, "Since, Father, I am still a minor, and children are taught to obey their parents, I will abstain from food or drink during the Fast, but only because you desire me to do so. In doing so I am going against my conscience, for I am saved through faith in the Lord Jesus, by the grace of God. I, therefore, cannot formulate the intention but, on the contrary, I daily renew my intention to trust in Jesus Christ alone for salvation. When I attain my majority and am free, then I intend to break the Fast. If you compel me to fast I will do so, but you will see that it has thus no value for me, either before God or to Muslims. God knows the real intention of my heart, for I am a Christian." '

This may not be the final answer to this thorny

problem, for it is a serious thing to teach a child or young person to disobey parents; but it is also a terrible thing to force anyone to disobey the dictates of conscience and the principles of the Word of God. The Christian missionary will never tell anyone not to fast. He will avoid giving rules, but he will point the convert to the principles of the Word of God. For the former Muslim these principles are clearly set forth in the Galatian epistle.

(iii) Prayer

'La illah ila Allah ...' (There is no god but God). The strident voice of the Muslim sheikh rang out through the still night air. Abd alMasih sat up on his bed and rubbed his eyes. He was sleeping in a Kabyle village and, judged by European standards, the bed was not a comfortable one, just a rush mat on which he had spread his sleeping sack after the previous day's long tramp. It was four o'clock and the voice of the muezzin continued, 'God is greater. God is greater. Prayer is better than sleep. Come to prayer. Come to prayer.'

The big wooden doors around opened, and dark forms found their way to the mosque. Curiosity drove Abd alMasih to rise and go down with them. He could not pray with them, but he could stand outside and watch. An early fall of snow had blanketed the whole village, but there was one pathway that stood out clearly in the snow. It was the path to the mosque, the only one that had been trodden so far. He watched each man arrive, carrying a small tin or jar for water. On arriving each man said, 'Oh God, I intend to pray the morning prayer. I witness that there is no other god than Allah and that He is without a partner, and I witness that Mohammed is His servant and His apostle.' Because a man must be ceremonially clean to pray each man then washed himself, his arms up to the elbow, his feet and his legs and other parts of his body, his face and neck and behind his ears. He also rinsed out his mouth. One late arrival merely rubbed his hands against the well-worn pillar of the mosque, and then went through the movements of washing, repeating the pious phrases.

Outside the mosque, shivering in the cold air stood two old women, watching the men, for they dare not go into the mosque to pray. Women might be unclean. Inside forty men stood in the dim light of an oil lamp, facing the east. In front of them stood the sheikh, and immediately before him was the *kiblah*, the niche in the wall that indicated the direction of Mecca. When the last man had joined the row, the prayer began:

'*God is great. There is no god but Allah, and Mohammed is his apostle. I take refuge in God from Satan the stoned . . .*'

Together they recited the first chapter of the Koran:

'*In the name of Allah, the Gracious, the Merciful. All praise belongs to Allah, Lord of all the worlds. The Gracious, the Merciful, Master of the Day of Judgement. Thee alone do we worship, and Thee alone do we implore for help. Guide us in the right path, the path of those on whom Thou hast bestowed Thy blessings, those who have not incurred Thy displeasure, and those who have not gone astray.*'

Out in the cold the two poor old women stood and mumbled the words.

The sheikh said, '*God is great*' and bent down until his forehead touched the ground. The men did the same after him. In this position they said,

'*Glory be to God the Lord of the Universe.*'

Then they stood and said,

'*God hears those who praise Him.*'

Three times they bowed themselves saying,

'*Glory to God the Lord most high.*'

Kneeling and raising their heads they cried, '*God is great*'. Then they recited,

'*Oh God, forgive me, have pity on me, direct me aright, preserve me and make me great. Strengthen my faith and enrich me . . .*'

So the prayer went on. The women watched from outside and went through exactly the same procedure. They longed to do right, but were shut out.

At last the prayer was finished. Each man turned his head, first to the right, then to the left, and saluted the angels saying the age-long formula,

'*Peace be unto you.*' '*Peace be unto you.*'

As Abd alMasih watched he was deeply moved. There was something uncanny, deeply mystical, yet profoundly impressing in this early morning prayer. He could not do otherwise than respect this solemn observance of prayer, the acknowledgement of the one God. For many of these men it expressed a true desire, a deep yearning for God. For some it was obviously just a formality, something to do. But for many others it was the expression of an intense thirst for God. As he made his way back to his host's house he reflected on the petitions. 'Lead us in the right way.' 'Forgive us.' 'Preserve me from evil.' He thought, too, of David's prayer, 'As the hart panteth after the unseen water brooks, so panteth my soul after Thee, O God. My soul thirsteth for God, the living God.' Here then was a thirst for God, a deep longing. But the true life-giving streams were hidden from their eyes. 'Lead us in the right way,' they had pleaded. But how could they know the way? There is only one Way back to God. 'Forgive us,' they had cried, but, 'without the shedding of blood there is no forgiveness.' Every single one of the blessings for which their soul yearned was found in Christ and in Him alone. And he, Abd alMasih, was here to tell them, to tell them of HIM.

As he reached the house his host called him to drink a cup of coffee which had been prepared. The fire burned brightly and over it was cooking a cake of unleavened bread on a griddle. As soon as it was cooked, Hamid took the bread, gave some to Abd alMasih and put some into his own bag. He opened the door of the courtyard to let out the two oxen. Carrying his rough wooden plough on his shoulder with the pointed goad in his hand, he descended to the plain where the snow would quickly melt. The next prayer time would be about one o'clock, then again at three, at sunset and one hour after that.

So, year in, year out, five times a day, this simple peasant man prays, spending an hour each day in his devotions. This is the *salat* or ritualistic prayer. There is also the *duwa* which approximates to the usual intercessory prayers of Christians. In this form of prayer the devotee holds out his hands before him with palms uplifted, level with his chest. When he has completed his prayer, he kisses the tips of his fingers and strokes his beard with the palms of his hands.

From the early days Abd alMasih saw that there was a fear of God in the hearts of these men. They boldly confessed their faith and witnessed to Mohammed, they fasted and they prayed.

(iv) Giving

From the very first Abd alMasih had been impressed by the generosity of the Kabyles. Even though he was an absolute stranger, they would offer a meal, a cup of coffee, or even hospitality for the night. If they were gathering walnuts when he passed through their village they would offer him fifty or a hundred nuts. If it was the fig time, the very best dried figs would be offered, and he would be invited to eat his fill of delicious green figs from the trees. Poor though they were, they would give of their best, for was he not a servant of God? He also found that while in this way they did undoubtedly express their gratitude for services rendered to them and for medicine, yet, to some extent, it was part of their religion. They were amassing merit, good deeds which would be put to their account for eternity.

For these Muslims alms-giving is of two classes, *zakat* which is obligatory, and *sadaqah*, which is a free will offering. Zakat is a levy on various kinds of property or income at fixed rates. These Muslims believe that God will repay the giver doubly and with interest. The freewill offerings are given from a man's personal property and earnings. As a traveller in the mountains, Abd alMasih was regarded as one of those to whom help should be extended. Others were the Muslim teachers, the poor, widows and orphans as well as those who were fighting for Islam. In offering hospitality to the Christian missionary they were gaining a reward, here and in Paradise.

He also discovered that, when they asked him to give them medicine or money, they were fully persuaded that they were conferring a boon on him! They were offering him the opportunity to acquire merit for himself. Just as they sought to give generously, and sometimes very ostentatiously, so should he. And this certainly explained to some extent their apparent lack of gratitude for so much that was done for them at the clinics. Was not the missionary acquiring merit through them? Let him then be grateful! '*Ror ek loujour, a sheikh*' ('You are getting a reward, o sheikh'), they repeated. A religion of works, of acquiring merit. This gradually penetrated his mind. How different their thoughts were from his!

(v) The Pilgrimage

One day Abd alMasih dropped in to see his old friend Si
Tahar. He was the policeman of the tribe, and had always
shown a real interest in the Word of God. Whenever Abd
alMasih was in his tribe he would call on Si Tahar, who
would always ask for a passage of the Bible to be read and
explained. It seemed that he might even be a believer –
albeit a secret believer – in the Lord Jesus. Today he was
strangely silent and reserved. Then it transpired that he
had just returned from the pilgrimage to Mecca. He was a
hajji.

'Why do you not wear a green turban to show that you
are a hajji?' enquired Abd alMasih.

'All that belongs to bygone days, sheikh. Few of us
wear it now.'

'Whatever made you go to Mecca? I thought that you
were too poor to afford to pay for the journey.'

'You know, sheikh, that I am an official and work for
France. Each year the French Government pays for some
of us to make the pilgrimage. You know that every Muslim must make the pilgrimage at least once in his life time.
Many do it three times. If a man can pay for the journey
and support his family while he is away, he should go. The
Administrator asked me if I would like to go. It cost me
nothing – or not very much – so I went.'

'Tell me all about it' said Abd alMasih.

Si Tahar was very reluctant to tell of what he had done
and seen but, after a time, he said, 'We left Algiers in the
boat that the Government had requisitioned. It was very
crowded, and we were not at all comfortable. It was very
hot. The boat was dirty. We travelled to Port Said, then
down the Suez Canal and through the Red Sea to the port
of Jiddah. That was where the real pilgrimage began. We
still had to travel across the desert and it was terribly hot.

Some travelled by camels, some by taxi and some by lorry or bus. I went on a lorry. A man can spend everything he possesses on drink. That is all you want to do – drink. There are no fountains such as we have in our mountains. You have to buy every drop of water and lemonade. Then at night you have to be very careful or some one will steal all your money. Of course, I was not alone, but no one there knew that I was a policeman. When we got near to the holy city we had to walk. That was the real pilgrimage.'

'Tell me a little more of what you did, what you saw.'

Si Tahar still seemed very reluctant but continued, 'When we were about ten kilometres from Mecca each of us put off his clothes and put on two seamless garments. After that we were in the state of *ihram*, holy or set apart. We were not allowed to shave or cut our hair. We visited the sacred mosque, kissed the black stone, and walked round and round the Kaaba (a temple). It was really wonderful and there were thousands of Muslims from all over the world. Islam is a worldwide religion, sheikh. Then we visited the sacred stone that they call *Maqam Ibrahim*. Some of the things that we had to do there were like what the old women and others do when they go to the tops of the mountains here in Kabylia and visit the holy places. At the very time when all Muslims throughout the world were killing the rams and thinking of how God sent a ram to our Lord Abraham to offer up instead of Ishmael, we offered a sacrifice.'

'But surely you could not eat the meat of a whole animal in the few days that you were there?'

'No, we ate some, and some we gave away, for there are thousands of beggars. I have never before seen so many.'

'Tell me something more of what you did.'

'Perhaps I will another day. But you need a lot of

money. What I spent in buying drinks and lemonade is no man's business.'

'That seems to have impressed you more than anything else,' said Abd alMasih. 'Now you are back, and I expect that you will proudly call yourself *alhajj*.'

'How can I be proud? I saw some things of which I shall always be ashamed. I would rather not tell you about them. But the Government sent me. I just went.'

'From now on shall I call you alhajj?'

'No sheikh. You should know the proverb that we have in Kabyle. "If a man has been on pilgrimage once, do not remain in the same house with him. If he has been to Mecca twice, do not stay in the same town. But if he has been three times you should not even stay in the same country." '

So, as he moved about among the people, Abd alMasih saw Islam in action. The five pillars of Islam composed this religion of works. Where did it come from? Mohammed copied it. It is an imitation of the true faith, yet everything is slightly twisted and warped. It is truth mingled with error. It is the weapon which Satan uses today to delude millions of people.

It is what a man does for God. And everything that man does for God must be imperfect. Abd alMasih had come to tell them what God has done for man. God's work is always perfect. That was the difference: Islam, what man does for God; the gospel, what God has done for man.

Chapter Six

Taking the Offensive

With increasing fluency in the languages there came a growing longing in Abd alMasih to reach out further with the message of life. Kabylia is a land of villages, and there are only two sizeable towns in the whole area, Tizi Ouzou in Greater Kabylia, and Bougie in Lesser Kabylia. There are also many Kabyles living in Algiers. The apostle Paul occupied the strategic towns and from them reached out to the smaller centres. The towns of Algeria had been occupied by missionaries for many years, but always their difficulty had been that of making and maintaining contact with individuals or groups of men. The lady missionary can always find an entrance to homes, but the men tend to congregate in the very large coffee houses and mosques of the towns, and in such places it is almost impossible to preach the gospel. In the villages, however, close contact could be made with the men.

The tribe of Beni Seliman (sons of Solomon), could be reached only by spending a night in one of their villages. Abd alMasih set out early one morning in his car, drove twenty miles along the road, and left it with a friendly French road maker, informing him that he would be back the next day. He packed a loaf of bread and his sleeping bag into his rucksack, in addition to some tracts and his New Testament. Quickly he dropped down to the ravine that was now lined with beautiful pink oleanders in full bloom. After fording the stream he began his long walk.

He arrived at the first village, so small that it really should be called a hamlet. The two dozen houses were grouped closely together, but not a man could be seen. Apparently everyone was in the fields. He dared not go to the houses, for young women should never even see a strange man, and the houses are guarded by fierce dogs. There are times when a little holy audacity pays very rich dividends. He took off his shoes at the entrance to the mosque and, climbing the minaret, he gave the call to prayer, studiously avoiding the name of the false prophet. That certainly shook them and brought the men from their homes. Within a few minutes he was surrounded by a group of curious and interested men.

This was the last village of the tribe, and to reach the next tribe meant a long walk of seven miles, climbing up a winding goat track to a height of 4,000 feet before dropping down on the group of villages that formed that particular tribe. The sun beat down on him as he trudged on with mixed feelings in his heart. There was the thrill of breaking up fresh ground, of going to those who had never heard, the compelling urge in his heart that drove him on, the knowledge that without Christ these men would die in their sins; yet, there was a lurking fear, a feeling of utter loneliness. What would be his reception in this new and unknown tribe? Where would he eventually spend the night? He knew no one, and there were no hotels or rest houses to which he could go.

As he neared the tribe he saw some of the older women at the fountain. They were washing their clothes, and filling their goat skins and pots with water. He was parched and dry. Standing some thirty yards from the fountain and turning his back on the women, he called, 'Oh, old woman, bring me to drink.' The oldest woman, an old hag, wrinkled with age, her hair dyed red with henna, brought him a pitcher full of water. Turning his head he said '*B ism Allah*' (In the name of God), and then drank his fill. When he had satisfied his thirst he said, 'Praise be to God,' and handed back the pitcher. There is quite an art in drinking from an earthen pitcher without actually touching it with one's lips, and without soaking one's shirt with water! He had long before learned that a man does not converse with a woman. When he passes a woman in the street, he gives no sign of recognition, even though he may know her well, or even have put her through a physical examination in the dispensary. A woman, whether veiled or not, always keeps her eyes down in public, and passes without speaking to a man while the man turns away his head. A man never addresses his wife directly in public, and never, never kisses her 'Goodbye' when he leaves her. All this is etiquette which must be learned.

Abd alMasih reached the village of elKoudia, a pictur-esque village with the red-tiled roofs showing up against the surrounding rocks and background of Aleppo pines. It was dominated by the mosque with a tall minaret. From this building came the low drone of voices repeating the Koran. He had never before been to this isolated village. Following the sound he came upon a group of thirty Koranic students, ranging in age from fifteen to twenty years. They were seated in a large room at one side of the mosque, their theological college, a veritable school of the prophets. Each one held a wooden slate on which he had written a passage of the Koran. They were repeating these passages, shouting them at the top of their voices, no two repeating the same passage. Yet their master, who sat in the centre of the ring with a long stick in his hand, could detect the slightest error in their reading. When he did so, he would touch the slate of the offending pupil with his stick. These are the most difficult of all people to approach. They are so proud, so bigoted, so unapproachable. Quite suddenly their teacher turned round and saw him. He rushed out, greeted him, kissed him on each cheek, warmly shaking his hand and bidding him welcome. But why this enthusiasm in a village which he had never before visited with the gospel?

'Surely you remember me, Abd alMasih? I brought my little daughter to your clinic. She was dying. You cared for her. You prayed with us. The return journey took us nearly seven hours. We shall never forget it, but God heard your prayers in the name of the Lord Jesus. He healed her. Today she is quite well. Welcome to our village and to our tribe.' A bright girlie with a colourful scarf round her head came running up.

'Look here she is, sheikh. Well and strong. To God be the praise! All thanks to you, Abd alMasih. Come and have dinner with me.'

'Thank you, O teacher,' Abd alMasih replied, 'but just one thing has brought me here. I have a message from God that I must deliver. Now please ask your students to put aside their slates. Give me just twenty minutes to tell them how they can find forgiveness for their sins. Then they can ask me questions.'

Koranic students are just like all theological students, anxious to demonstrate their skill in debate. For twenty minutes they listened to Abd alMasih as he sat with a chart of The Two Ways spread before him, showing them that Christ alone is the Way, the Truth and the Life, that He alone can remove the burden of sin. Many questions were asked before the Muslim sheikh took him home to his house. There his wife had prepared a meal. She had broken a dozen eggs into a dish, added some fine semolina and cooked the whole in hot olive oil. making a delicious omelette which was dripping with oil. Abd alMasih was hungry after his long walk and did justice to the meal. Having chatted for some time with the sheikh, he pushed on to the next village.

Zakoo was a large village and the men had gathered in the roomy coffee house well outside the village. As usual, the men sat round their low tables playing. Abd alMasih greeted them. One of them turned to him and said, 'If you have come only to tell us not to steal and lie and kill, then you can go away, for our sheikhs tell us that. But if you can tell us how to follow the good and avoid the evil, then say on.' A message on Romans 7:18–25 followed. It was heard attentively, the men leaving their games to listen.

The message finished, Abd alMasih rose to leave. One of the men also rose and came over to him. He said, 'I have a question to ask, sheikh; tell me, how would you like to spend a whole year with just one meal?' Abd alMasih had to agree that it would be rather a long time to fast. The man continued, 'In this village we are hungry. Our hearts are hungry. We long for some spiritual satisfaction, an assurance of forgiveness. Our religion does not satisfy our hearts. Dominoes and cards do not give us that inward satisfaction for which we crave. The words that you read from that Book go right down into our hearts. Yet you come so seldom. One meal a year.'

Abd alMasih thought hard. He had never been to that village before, and it was several years since he had been to the neighbouring tribe where some of those men had met him. He had visited nearly one hundred and fifty villages the preceding year, and only twenty of these were on a road; two hundred and thirty-five visits had been paid, but these were on the fringe of his wide field. To reach them meant travelling for many hours, way out among the hills. Yet there were people who lived in the homeland who said it was impossible to evangelise Muslims!

Leaving Zakoo, Abd alMasih climbed up to a little knoll that overlooked the valley. There were nine villages in this tribe and he had already reached two. One more could be reached that evening. Already the smoke was arising from the houses as the women prepared the evening meal. He lifted his heart to God to guide him to the right place to spend the night. So much depended on the friendly or hostile attitude of the people in that last village.

He wended his way to the largest village, and found the men gathered in the thejmath, the equivalent of the gateway of the village. There the village elders gather to discuss the affairs of the community; fines are imposed on those who transgress the local laws. Nearby was the mosque, but the sheikh remained discreetly hidden. News quickly spread that a stranger who knew Kabyle had arrived. The men were seated on the stone benches that lined each side of the thejmath; behind them sat the younger men, while in the background a group of boys craned their necks to see. The whole male population was there. One poor man was quite obviously suffering from violent toothache. Two days previously he had visited the local blacksmith, who had endeavoured to extract the tooth with his home-made forceps, but had broken it off at the gums leaving the roots in. Abd alMasih examined the tooth and realised that the roots could now be extracted. He could use no anaesthetic, but the roots came out in one piece, to the obvious approval of the onlookers. Immediately a long queue of men and boys wanted teeth extracted, but time was passing and they were asked to wait until the morning. It was important to get over a message before sunset. He resumed his seat among the men.

'May God be merciful to your forefathers', said one.

'May He forgive you your sins, if He wills,' echoed another. Abd alMasih saw his opportunity.

'Praise be to God, He has forgiven me,' he said.

'No one can know that,' said an old man.

'How can we really know that God has forgiven our sins?' chimed in another.

Deep in the heart of every Muslim is this strong desire for the assurance of salvation. His religion is a religion of works. He believes that at the Last Day God will balance his good works against the bad, and not until then will he know that he is forgiven. But five times a day he repeats, 'O God, have mercy on me and forgive me.' Scores of times each day he says, '*Asterofer Allah*' (I ask pardon of God), but if anyone asks him if he has found pardon he will reply, 'I do not know. If God wills . . .' Abd alMasih read to them the story of the paralysed man from Luke 5:

'Son, thy sins be forgiven thee . . . That you may know that the Son of man hath power on earth to forgive sins.' He reminded them of the sacrifices of olden times, of the story of Genesis 22, of the red heifer, and that 'without the shedding of blood there is no remission.' Finally he read to them Acts 10: 'To Him all the prophets witness that whosoever believes in Him shall receive remission of sins.'

The sheikh's voice rang out from the nearby mosque, calling the faithful to prayer. Not a man responded. They continued to listen to the message. Questions were asked. Fully ten minutes later some men left to pray. A man came up to Abd alMasih and said, 'Come.' He followed him until they reached a large oak door which was richly carved with oriental designs. This opened on to a large courtyard flagged with stones. A few sheep in one corner munched at some branches of a tree that had been cut off and brought in. His host shouted the name of his eldest son, a child of five, and his wife ran to open the door. 'Welcome to our house,' said Ali, his host. Fathema, his wife, ran up, pulled down the head of Abd alMasih and kissed him on his beret. She had been to the dispensary for treatment. Then she sprinkled some water around and started to sweep the floor. A mat was thrown down, Abd alMasih slipped off his boots and, dead tired, stretched himself on the mat.

The soup was cooking on the fire in a large earthen pot, over which was placed a sort of colander. This was filled with *couscous*, the staple food of the Kabyles, which the steam, percolating through the holes, cooked. Couscous is made from semolina or wheat flour which has been rolled into small grains. The soup is made of onions, lentils, beans or peas and is highly seasoned with spices and pepper. Abd alMasih watched as Fathema removed the cloth band which was wrapped round the two parts of the cooking pot to prevent the steam escaping. Taking some strips of dried meat, which looked suspiciously like leather, from a bowl of water, she slipped them into the soup. It must be remembered that Abd alMasih was an almost total stranger to these people, that he arrived late in the day, and was entirely unexpected. Their hospitality to strangers puts many Christians to shame.

Half an hour later Fathema removed the colander holding the couscous, and emptied it into the *tharbouth* (a large wooden bowl about thirty inches in diameter and four inches deep, hewn from a solid trunk of a tree by hand). With a deft movement of her hands, Fathema anointed the couscous, using butter on this occasion as a special treat. Usually strong olive oil is used. Then she piled up the couscous on to another large wooden dish, and stuck a series of wooden spoons into it.

'Draw near and eat' said Ali. He and his two sons and a cousin, who had come in from next door, squatted round the dish. Abd alMasih squatted with them. Each man scooped out a little hole in the mass of couscous, and Ali poured some soup with lentils and beans into each hole. The lumps of meat were placed on top. Everything looked very clean. Then father said '*B ism Allah*' (in the name of God), and all started to eat.

Kabyle men and boys always eat their fill first, and this family was true to type. Fathema hovered around in the background within call, but almost unseen in the shadows. When all had finished eating, Ali said, 'Have some more.'

'I have had enough,' Abd alMasih replied.

'Do not be ashamed of eating more. Eat,' said Ali.

'Thank you, I have had enough. Praise the Lord.'

'Swear you have had enough,' said Ali.

A Kabyle will never clear up all the food from the plate, but leave quite a lot to show that he is really satisfied. To clear one's plate would be the very essence of bad manners.

The remainder of the food was then passed on to Fathema and the two little girls. No meat was left for them. They were glad indeed to be able to share the couscous. In many rural areas, where barley is the staple food, the women are given only the outer husk of the barley, a mixture that many fowls in England would refuse to eat.

Supper ended, father, the boys and the neighbour drew the hoods of their large woollen burnouses over their heads, and reclined on their elbows round the glowing embers of the fire. The woman and girls squatted behind in the shadows and one could just discern their faces in the light of the old fashioned lamp. In this remote village it was difficult to obtain paraffin, so a rough wick floated in olive oil in an earthenware lamp. The lamp had to be replenished with oil every half-hour or so, and it gave a smoky fluttering flame. But this was just enough to enable Abd alMasih to read the New Testament. He took not the slightest notice of the woman and girls. He did not speak to them. They did not speak to him. As he read he was most careful to utter no word that would give offence. He avoided all reference to sins of the flesh, even in an indirect way. He knew that to read the word adultery in a public meeting would be to lose the entire audience. How much more so here! In the very early days he had read the story of the woman in Simon's house who anointed the Lord's feet with oil and wiped them with the hairs of her head. His host showed him quite plainly that to read such a passage with the women of the family present was to be guilty of a breach of etiquette. That woman in Simon's house showed her character too plainly and to read this to a family was to throw some doubt on the moral character of the women present.

As Abd alMasih spoke of the Son of God Who loved them and died for them, he felt that God was present. How very like a scene from the New Testament it was! Jesus Himself drew near. The message finished, they fell to talking and many thoughtful questions were asked and answered. There was no banter, no questions to ward off the essentials, but a spirit of enquiry. He suggested that he might ask God's blessing on His Word and on this house, to which Ali heartily agreed. Each one present stretched out his hands, palms upwards in true Old Testament style, as Abd alMasih sought God's blessing on the household in the Name of the Lord Jesus. The neighbour said 'Good-night' and rose to go. Ali followed him out, closing and barring the courtyard door. Then he came in, closing and barring the door of the house. It would not be opened till morning, and no one would be expected to go out or come in until then. Throughout the day it would remain open. Ali alone had the right to open or shut that door.

Meanwhile Fathema had spread more mats, the children had fallen asleep and were rolled in their blankets. Then Ali turned to Abd alMasih and said, 'I should like you to examine my wife, and give her the necessary treatment.' She stretched out on the mat and covered herself with a rug. It was evidently venereal disease.

Abd alMasih unpacked his sleeping bag and prepared

his bed. Both husband and wife were most interested. They offered blankets and even a dirty sheet which he modestly declined. He laid his sleeping bag on the rush mat covering the mud floor, and snuggled into it. The others stretched out around him, the light was extinguished and he sought to sleep. Just behind him the two cows peacefully chewed the cud throughout the night. A dozen goats imparted a decided relish to the atmosphere, as well as contributing numerous small insects. These seemed to concentrate their undivided attention on the poor foreigner with the tender skin. He settled down to rest, if not to sleep, and listened to the fitful snores of his host as he tossed in his dirty verminous blankets.

Abd alMasih was not altogether sorry when the crowing of the cock perched above his head announced that a new day was breaking. Ali brought him some soap and a cupful of water. He poured a little over his hands and made a lather with which he washed his face. Then Ali poured out the water a little at a time over the back of his neck while he rinsed off the lather. He found how refreshing it was to have a wash in half a pint of water, after spending a night in a Kabyle house. A cup of coffee followed, and he bade farewell to his host.

Finding his way to the meeting place Abd alMasih gave another message. Many teeth and roots had to be extracted, some fifty-three in all. Then one man after another took him to his home for more teeth extractions. He finally turned his face homewards, calling at a number of villages on the way. These village gatherings, the large evening meeting when over one hundred were present, and the intimate family group around the fire, made such repeated efforts more than worthwhile.

Learning the Koran

A village meeting

*Teeth extraction
after the meeting*

Chapter Seven

Never Knocked Out

'We are handicapped on all sides, but we are never frustrated. We are puzzled, but never in despair. We are persecuted, but we never have to stand alone. We may be knocked down, but are never knocked out!' (2 Corinthians 4:8,9 [Phillips]).

The missionary to Muslims is acutely conscious that he faces a powerful adversary. Like a skilled boxer, who rains blow after blow on his opponent's body, each one intended to be a knock-out blow, Satan attempts to stop the work of God time and again. But, like Paul, the missionary never gives up, he never gives in. He gets up and continues the fight, only to realise that God, in His overruling and all-wise providence makes these knock-out blows the means to fresh avenues of service. How well this is exemplified throughout the life and service of Paul!

It was never intended that Lafayette should be a mission station, but rather a centre from which the gospel could radiate to the surrounding tribes. At the same time, Lalla Jouhra and Abd alMasih were conscious of a tremendous spiritual need in the place where they lived, both among Muslims and Europeans. They started a class for girls and another for boys. These were held in their living room and, by the end of the class, the furniture was often thick with mud. Each Sunday fifteen to twenty French people attended the gospel meeting. It was delightful for the mission people to have their own home, and to be able to use it for the Lord's work even though it was only three rooms and a kitchen, plus a toilet in a public yard, to reach which involved a walk of one hundred yards up the street! The living room served as dining room, classroom, meeting room for gospel services and a reception room for visitors.

They could never forget the first visit of the local R.C. priest. He was nearly as inexperienced as they were! After a little preliminary conversation, Abd alMasih referred to John 1.12 and offered the good man a Bible; whereupon he proceeded to turn over the pages of Genesis in an attempt to find the Gospel of John. Then on to Exodus and a jump to the Psalms.

'Can I help you, Monsieur le curé?' said Abd alMasih. He found John 1:12 and a most interesting talk ensued.

The priest left, and, meeting the headmaster of the school, said, 'These people are going to destroy all my work and take all my flock. What shall I do?'

The teacher replied, 'Surely, if it is you who teach the truth, then you have no cause for anxiety but, if on the contrary, they are right, what do you expect? You will lose your flock.'

The next day the schoolmaster's wife sent for a Bible. She also started to attend the gospel meetings which at that time were well frequented by a number of Roman Catholics. The priest heard of her interest and invited himself to tea, saying that he too would like to see a Protestant Bible. She handed it to him. Without further ado he left the house, without even saying 'Farewell,' and taking the Bible with him. Returning home the schoolmaster was furious, and sent to say that he was prepared to prosecute the priest for the theft of a book from his library. Abd alMasih pleaded with him to do no such thing. The schoolmaster did write to the priest asking that the Bible be returned at once, and warning him of the consequences of a refusal. A letter came by return of post. The priest said that he was so sorry not to be able to return the Bible, but this was quite impossible. He had burned it the previous day!

The sequel came several months later when the Protestant bus driver was talking with the hotel keeper in the priest's village. The conversation turned to missionaries.

'We do not know them, but we have one of their Bibles in which their name is marked. It seems to be a good book. Look, here it is.'

'Tell me,' replied the bus driver, 'Where did you get this?'

'The priest sold it to me for thirty francs.'

'Do you know that you could buy a new copy for ten francs?'

Thank God those days are past, and today Roman Catholics are allowed to read the Bible. The evil one had sought to deal a knock-out blow through the priest, and stop the work, but, by the grace of God, it was parried. There was more to come.

The Roman Catholics continued to attend the gospel meetings, and eventually the wife of the missionaries' landlord, an immoral woman, was converted. Fearful lest she should be really converted, the landlord determined to expel the missionaries from the village. He sold the house over their heads, and they received notice to quit. They could not find even one room in which to live. God's work was going on so well. They had succeeded in making contact with so many Muslims, scores of children were attending the classes. Many homes were open. Contacts had been made with men. God was working. Then the blow fell. Notice to quit. They were homeless. Put out on the street with no right of appeal. In fellowship with their Lord they had nowhere to lay their heads. The French judge was exceedingly kind and found them a house in an Arab village, six miles away, but they did not know Arabic, only French and Kabyle. With heavy hearts they loaded their few belongings on to a lorry, and set off for this village where they would be the only Europeans. It was the most fanatical Muslim village of the whole area. How depressed and downcast they felt as they said 'Goodbye' to their first home!

The place to which God, in His infinite wisdom, took them was called Hammam. Although its inhabitants were now almost all Arabs, a few Kabyle women were married to Arab men. There Abd alMasih tackled his fourth language. He started a dispensary, classes for boys and meetings for men. Soon crowds of people were coming for treatment. As knowledge of the language increased, so did numbers. The Lord's blessing rested on the work even in those early days. Souls were saved. For thirty-five years the Lord's work was continued in that fanatical centre. As many as 8,000 patients were treated each year, and the gospel message was spread over a wide area. To this strategic centre the Lord sent them, and to do so He used what Satan intended as a knock-out blow! Satan is strong, but God is Sovereign. He is All-wise and Almighty. He makes all things to work together for good to those who love Him. But the knock-out blows are hard.

The village of Hammam proved to be a most interesting place. Extensive Roman ruins were a continual reminder that in the early centuries of the Christian era this place had been the seat of two bishoprics, Romanist and Donatist. A stone bearing the names of twelve men who had been martyred for their Christian faith reminded them that many early Christians, who had been faithful to their Lord, had suffered for it. In the mountains behind the village extensive underground passages and catacombs were to be found, telling of those who were driven underground because they loved the Lord. How these corridors must have echoed with the hymns and praises of those who sang the songs of Zion! The hot radioactive waters had been exploited by the Romans centuries before. They had constructed extensive and elaborate public baths (Hammam means bath) the remains of which could be clearly seen, and some of which were still in use. For most of the year, but especially during the spring and summer months, large crowds of sick folk flocked for healing to this thermal centre, many of them from long distances. It was soon evident that this was a strategic centre, and it was up to Abd alMasih and Lalla Jouhra to exploit this new situation.

The population soon discovered that Abd alMasih had some knowledge of medicine and quickly appealed to him for help. The one French Doctor, for a population of over 100,000, lived several miles away. It was quickly evident that by caring for the sick and seeking to alleviate suffering, the missionaries could not only render service to people, but give some tangible evidence of their concern for them. The whole population was Muslim, most of them being of the Marabout or priestly caste. It was known that they were religious fanatics who would persistently oppose and persecute any who became Christian. But the Lord Jesus had said, 'Love your enemies, do good to them that hate you.' He Himself had exercised a healing ministry. He was moved with compassion by the sight of crowds of sick and suffering people, and He healed them all. When He sent out His disciples He gave them power to heal all manner of sickness and all manner of disease. Practical love is a most effective weapon in the spiritual warfare.

At this time Abd alMasih and Lalla Jouhra were extending their outreach to the villages and the homes. It was much more difficult to induce the people to come to them, and to gather in a place where they could listen quietly to the message. How could they persuade men to come? The answer was a small dispensary where those who were sick could find relief and healing, and which the timid and reticent could use as an excuse for attending. They had not the training, or the resources, to open a hospital, but in the dispensary they would be able to devote more time and energy to the spiritual side of the work. So Abd alMasih announced that twice a week the sick would be cared for in the garage adjoining their house.

As Abd alMasih moved about among the people he was horrified to see the suffering brought about through ignorance, neglect and the absence of a skilled practitioner. The people had their own crude methods of caring for the sick and injured, but all too often they only aggravated the pain and suffering. In one isolated village he found a boy with a compound fracture of the radius. This had been 'set' by a Kabyle bone-setter. Four small pieces of wood six inches long and one inch wide had been bound tightly round the arm. The hand and the arm above the wound had swollen to twice their normal size, and the tissues immediately surrounding the wound had shrunk. The ends of the bone had pierced the skin and were rubbing against the splints. The whole was a suppurating mass which had been covered with a black sticky preparation resembling tar. The stench was unbearable, and the poor lad had been in this state for nearly a month.

How ignorant are some of the poor women! A baby boy was afflicted with measles. As is so often the case, eye trouble developed and no medical advice was available. The women neighbours prescribed that the mother should take glass and grind it to a fine powder with a stone; then lifting the lids she should pour the ground glass into each eye, rubbing it in by diligent massage; the baby would scream, but she should persist, even if the eyes bled freely. The tragedy is that the poor ignorant mother implicitly followed their instructions and blinded her son for life.

In order to arrest haemorrhage, they often plaster the wound with a mixture of cow manure and antimony. This aggravates the lesion, pus accumulates and, being unable to escape, the wound swells and finally bursts. To clean up such a wound before applying a dressing, required boundless patience and skill.

A favourite remedy to reduce inflammation or oedema is cauterisation. A sickle is heated until it is red hot, and the point is then repeatedly applied to the swollen member until the whole area is covered with a series of small burns. This remedy is often used on babies; it is reputed to make them strong! At times a red hot needle is pushed right into the skin and flesh, a piece of unsterilised string being then inserted in the hole so made and left in position to act as a drain.

At the mosque in Hammam the boys learn the Koran from wooden slates which are coated with whiting or chalk. The chapter of the Koran which is to be memorized is copied on to the slate with a pen made from a split reed. This is dipped in ink made from charred sheep's wool and gum. The water used to wash the slate clean is called the 'Holy water' and is kept in a large earthen jar outside the mosque. It is reputed to be a certain remedy for many complaints. The patients drink it and this, of course, is equivalent to drinking the Word of God!

To cure indigestion or dyspepsia a man is grasped by the throat and throttled until his face turns blue and he is unconscious. Dizziness often accompanies anaemia, and this is cured by tying the patient's ankles together and then suspending him, or her, head downwards from the central beam of the house. The patient is left in this position for an hour or more. A certain cure for the common cold is to drink a gill of paraffin!

When a mother-to-be has been in labour for some time, delivery is hastened by rolling a heavy log over her abdomen, or by a woman jumping on her tummy.

Eye troubles abound. Native doctors operate in a crude way for cataracts. They incise the eyeball, and extract the cataract like a pea; in some fifty per cent of the cases the operation succeeds. In many areas almost the whole population suffers from trachoma, or granular lids. This often leads to in-growing eyelashes. The continual friction of the lashes against the eyeball irritates the eye and eventually leads to opaqueness of the cornea and blindness.

One patient was suffering from corneal ulcers. He came with a most peculiar contraption over his head. The Arab doctor had treated him for in-growing eyelashes. The outside skin of the upper eyelids had been compressed between two small pieces of stick. These had been tightly bound together by thread. This caused the skin of the lid to slough away, subsequently forming scar tissue, so that the eyelashes were drawn away from the cornea. While undergoing this treatment the patient's eyes were kept open by pieces of string tied back over his head to a sort of collar round his neck. He had been unable to close his eyes for a month, and corneal ulcers had developed. The principle was good, but the means taken were cruel and involved terrible suffering for the patient.

In the early days of the service of Abd alMasih and Lalla Jouhra smallpox was very prevalent, especially in the more isolated villages. In one place about thirty men and boys gathered on the village square, all afflicted with purulent smallpox. As the message was given rain started to fall. The men were covered from head to foot with large festering sores, and many of them were in the grip of a violent fever. Their wounds were covered with swarms of flies, and those who were strong enough to do so attempted to drive them away with a swatter made from a cow's tail. Suddenly a voice called from a nearby hut, 'Father, come and help me. Take me to be cured.' A twelve-year-old boy was carried out on a pallet. He was a frightful sight, the sores over his whole body were confluent and had formed a purulent mass. Flies swarmed to and fro. He pleaded for help. What could be done? It was too late to hope for a cure. He would soon pass into eternity. What simple remedies Abd alMasih had were passed on and the gospel was told in all its simplicity. For the first time in their lives, and for many the last time, those men and boys heard of eternal life, a hope after death, of the love of God Who forgives. The poor women were just left in the houses to suffer and die. No one cared for them.

It may well be that the reader is filled with revulsion by merely reading these things. A servant of God moving about among the people is continually brought face to face with such filth and suffering, much of which is caused by ignorance and lack of hygiene. If he did nothing to help relieve them he would be almost inhuman. He brings the message of salvation for the soul, but he must do something to help relieve suffering bodies.

For the first few months treatment was given in the garage, but this very soon proved to be inadequate. Crowds flocked to the newly opened dispensary. The news went round very quickly.

'Free medicine.' 'People get better quickly.'

'This new doctor fears God. He prays with us and for us. God heals us.'

'I went to him and it was there that I met God. God spoke to me there.'

'He does not turn any away. You go and see . . .'

So quickly did the news circulate, and so rapidly did numbers increase that the supply of medicines was quickly exhausted. Abd alMasih had no money to buy more. There was only one thing for him to do, tell his heavenly Father. So he bowed in prayer and placed the need before Him who never fails. The postman's knock surprised him for letters were only delivered once a week in this Arab village and this was not his day. The letter bore the postmark of Torquay and contained a gift of ten pounds for the medical work. Although Abd alMasih knew no one at Torquay, his Father did, and he had placed the need on the heart of this unknown donor. 'Before they call, I will answer.'

The weeks passed by; once more supplies were short; an order was made out and addressed to a wholesale firm of chemists. Abd alMasih hesitated to despatch that order as there was no money in hand, nothing with which to foot the bill. He left for market, and when he returned found a letter waiting for him. He opened the letter. Again there was a gift for the purchase of drugs. There was enough to pay the bill, plus the carriage of the box from Algiers, and . . . one halfpenny over!

The people appreciated the work so much that they placed a room at the disposal of Abd alMasih at a very nominal rent. Twice weekly a clinic was held in this large upper room over a coffee house. It was conveniently situated near the Baths and yet quite detached, with the door giving on to a yard where the women could wait. Let us then take a glance at this work.

Abd alMasih usually arrives soon after 7 a.m. to find a crowd of some forty or fifty patients waiting. Some have travelled since the early hours of the morning, leaving their homes in the night in order to arrive in time. The floor of the room is covered with rough mats, and several benches have been arranged in order to seat the maximum number. The women scuttle in first and take the back seats, arranging themselves so that just one eye is visible from beneath each veil. For many of them it is the only outing they will have during the whole year – their annual bath! The men then fill up the remainder of the available space, and the meeting begins. The story of the paralysed man is read from Luke 5, the message being illustrated by flannelgraph, emphasis being placed on the phrase, 'Son, thy sins be forgiven thee'. Then the truth is pressed home that 'without the shedding of blood there is no remission'. The story of the Cross follows. The message is followed intently. One man unconsciously rises to his feet. 'Sit down,' his friends shout at him. 'I did not want to miss a word of the message,' he said. Prayer is then made in the Lord's Name. It is deeply affecting to see these dear Muslims holding out their hands with palms extended upwards during the prayer. This attitude of prayer, copied from the believers of Old Testament days, indicates that they desire to receive the blessing asked for in the name of the Lord Jesus. The prayer concludes. There are many loud *Amens*, and some kiss the palms of their hands, and then slowly stroke their chins and chests with their fingers. The testimony of one poor 'shut-in' woman given years later was, 'If ever in my life I met God it was in that dispensary'.

There are those who think that the missionary should care for the body without giving a gospel message. They insist that it is unfair to take advantage of weakness or sickness to communicate the message of life. Throughout the years Abd alMasih and others have always sought to give a spiritual message to the patients before commencing treatment. Hundreds have been reached in this way, and God has been given first place. Man is a complex being. To care for his bodily ailments only and ignore the needs of his soul is illogical. Physical, mental and spiritual ailments are often closely linked. To heal a man's body and to withhold from him the message that alone can save his soul is almost criminal. The Lord sent His servants to preach the gospel, and obedience to His command means that they must do everything in their power to reach all. As servants of God they are answerable to Him for the eternal welfare of those with whom they come into contact. With Paul they can say, 'Woe is me if I preach not the gospel. Necessity is laid upon me.'

On one occasion, having cared for over a hundred patients single-handed, and given two half-hour messages, Abd alMasih felt completely exhausted.

'I will just care for those of you who remain,' he said to the men. 'I will give you medicine without a message from God's Word.'

'But why do you think that we come to you instead of going to the *tebib*?' they said. 'It is only because you fear God and ask Him to heal us and He does. If there is no message, O sheikh, then you must at least pray with us in the Name of the Lord Jesus.'

Tired though he was, Abd alMasih felt that he must accede to their request. He gave a short message and prayed.

The message ended, treatment of the men then begins. Says the first man, 'I had my whole body covered with a very bad skin disease. It lasted for twelve years. I went to many doctors in France, and in every large city in Algeria, but all treatment failed until I came to you. Now I am completely healed. God is with you. I believe in the Lord Jesus. I have brought these three men from my village. We left home at three o'clock this morning.'

The next man has severe malaria, and an injection of quinine is given. Another suffers from very severe indigestion. Each day his friends have almost strangled him in their well-intentioned efforts to cure him. A good purge and a dose of sodium bicarbonate soon put him right. A case of conjunctivitis is followed by a man with acute bronchitis. The man strips to the waist, and Abd alMasih examines him with his stethoscope and gives him medicine from the stock bottle. One after the other the men and boys are treated. The women wait behind. The men are not allowed to look around in curiosity to see who is there! It is eyes front, and those who do not conform are asked to leave.

When the last man has been treated and left, the door is shut and bolted, the veils come off, and treatment of the ladies proceeds. The first is a lady who has eaten nothing for five days. She is white and emaciated. Rising during the night to drink from a pitcher, she had swallowed a horse leech in the water, and the horrible creature had attached itself firmly to the back of the throat behind the nose. The body of the leech was just discernible like a big black swollen slug. All efforts to dislodge it had failed, and the poor woman was daily growing weaker through loss of blood. With the aid of a pair of artery forceps and a tongue depressor, the leech is removed, a styptic is applied and the haemorrhage is arrested. The poor young woman is intensely grateful. Her husband will be too; a new wife costs a lot of money!

The next woman holds a baby in her arms and throws back the shawl. The baby screams as the mother removes a filthy blood-stained rag from its head. She explains that she had left the baby for a moment in its cot, and had run in to speak to a neighbour. Snow was on the ground, the door was open, and to keep baby warm she had suspended the cot just near the fire. The baby, a lovely little girl, wrapped in tight swaddling clothes had wriggled and wriggled and eventually had fallen head first into the fire. The hair was almost completely burned away, together with a large part of the scalp and skin. The bones of the skull shone through the mass of tar-like substance that had been plastered on it. This case looked hopeless. The mother refused to allow the child to go to hospital. However, patient and persistent care triumphed, meningitis did not develop and the child lived to become a delightful girl even although she must always cover her head with a scarf, being quite bald. There are no wigs in the mountains!

The next is a woman with an axillary abscess which should have been excised days ago. Taking all possible precautions, the abscess is opened, the pus drained into a bowl and a dressing applied. Then a tooth is extracted, a case of malaria treated, and a dozen children with suppurating eyes dealt with. A mother asks for medicine for her little girl who is almost at death's door with diarrhoea and vomiting. Cases of T.B., skin diseases, dysentery and coughs follow. A woman desires treatment for abdominal pains. She is deeply concerned that she has never had a baby.

The last two patients are girls of fourteen, already young women in this land, and soon to be given in marriage. They are allowed to leave their homes only when they are accompanied by a male relative. He is waiting outside, and they are now in the care of an old woman. The veils are removed. What a sight they are. They dread the light. Conjunctivitis has been neglected and trachoma has developed. If this is not treated it will go on to cause opaqueness of the cornea and eventual blindness. The eyes are very swollen and painful. Already there is a white skin growing over the centre of each eye. They are treated, and take away ointment and eye drops for use at home. They must return twice a week for treatment for a considerable time. This really pleases them, for they are glad to escape from their seclusion, and Abd alMasih hopes that through regular attendance at the meetings the light may shine into their sin-blinded hearts.

Now nearly fifty others wait their turn outside. They have waited for three hours already. The European doctor has meanwhile been down with his beautifully equipped mobile clinic, offering immediate and free treatment to all who will avail themselves of it. He has had six patients, and left.

'Hurry up, sheikh,' says a man to Abd alMasih. 'We left home early this morning and have travelled for more than four hours to get here.'

'The doctor was available. Why did you not go to him? Treatment is free.'

'Sheikh, we know that you love us, we trust you, and above all you fear God. You pray for us and with us. You tell us about God. That is why we come to you. But these two veiled women who have come with me are getting tired of waiting!'

Once more the room is filled to capacity, the men in front and women behind. Another message, prayer, and treatment begins. The first patient is a man with a dislocated jaw. He has walked for four hours and has had nothing to eat for three days. He can only mumble and is in pain.

'Give him a sharp blow on the chin, sheikh,' says another man. Abd alMasih puts him in a chair in the corner where his head is immobilised. He wraps a towel round the thumbs of each hand, remembers the instructions given at Livingstone College so long ago. He grasps the man's lower jaw firmly, exerts steady downward pressure, back, round and up. With a click the jaw slips back into place. A murmur of approval goes up from the onlookers.

'May God be merciful to your forefathers.'

'May He give you many more children, and multiply your family.'

'May God bless you and multiply your good.' The man

gently feels his jaw, moves it up and down, a big grin spreads over his face! Next patient please. So the work goes on.

'Hit me with a needle, I have fever.'

'I have a frog in my throat,' complains another.

'My tummy goes up and down like this, and then round and round like this,' says one old man, demonstrating with his hands.

'Listen to the worms moving round in my tummy,' says another and he allows us to listen to the gurgle!

Again the men have all been treated and have left. The ladies remain, most of whom are young. Many have some sort of abdominal trouble. One old lady seems to be in great pain. She hobbles to the front.

'I was feeding the mule when it stepped back and trod on my toe,' she said. The mule had trodden so hard that the toe was almost severed. It was quite easy to amputate it, to apply medicine and a bandage. In a Kabyle house, where the animals share the limited space, such accidents often happen.

Abd alMasih often obtained an insight into the private lives of the people, enabling him to understand their customs, the bondage of the women, and the superstitions which dominate their lives. He was often helped in this way to apply the gospel to their needs and their circumstances.

One old man of over eighty years of age was found to have taken a new wife every year in a vain attempt to have children and to prevent his name and his family from becoming extinct. Many of these wives had been young girls. At the time he had two wives, one a girl of fourteen. Only financial reasons prevented him from taking the four wives that are allowed to every Muslim with as many concubines as he can support. This old man must have had at least sixty consecutive wives, but in vain. There were no children.

The more ignorant people always seek a quick cure. They will sometimes drink a whole bottle full of medicine at one draught. One man sent his little daughter for medicine. He was suffering from a violent headache and severe fever. The French have a lotion they call '*Eau Sedative*', and the older people appreciate this as it often quickly relieves their headaches. Abd alMasih gave the girl some tablets of aspirin, a purge and a bottle of Eau Sedative, with strict instructions as to how each was to be used. The man decided that he would like to get better in the shortest possible time. He swallowed all the tablets and the two pills, washing them down with all the lotion. The next day he was completely cured!

The Muslim is a born fatalist. One of the best known words in his language is *Mektoub* (It is decreed). He will defer treatment till the last possible moment, hoping against hope for a cure.

Perhaps the women suffer more than the men because of this fatalistic attitude, this unwillingness to seek advice and treatment. 'Sheikh, have you anything in your bag to help my wife. She is feeding a baby, but one breast is four times the size of the other. Come and see her.' Normally Abd alMasih did not carry drugs or medicines with him, but he always took a scalpel and one or two instruments. The poor woman was suffering terribly. She had not slept for nights because of the pain. The breast was distended to many times its normal size, the whole organ was tense, the axillary glands swollen. The woman was running a temperature and there was a very real danger of septicaemia. The only thing to do was to incise the abscess. Preparing the scalpel, Abd alMasih stood behind the poor women and plunged it in. With a scream she darted away, completing the work that he had started. The abscess was well and truly opened. The confined pus spurted out and hit the roof. The cleaning-up process was exceedingly painful, for the adjacent sections of the breast were infected and had to be broken down for the pus to be drawn off. Dressings were applied, a sedative given, and before he left the woman was sound asleep. The next day she travelled to the clinic for further treatment. Rushing in after her long journey, she pulled the missionary's head down and kissed him repeatedly. Then she kissed the hand that had held the scalpel. Her gratitude was boundless. The treatment was crude, but efficacious, and while many are utterly ungrateful, yet often a man or woman is deeply appreciative.

Back in his home Abd alMasih prepared stock medicines for the next dispensary day, for he was not only doctor and nurse, but chemist, dispenser and dentist.

Teeth were extracted at any time – a man or woman suffering from severe toothache cannot be made to wait several days. One day there was a knock at the front door. Lalla Jouhra opened it. A man with a very swollen jaw, who was obviously in great pain, stood outside. Very timidly he asked, 'Is the sheikh at home? I want him to take my tooth out.' 'I am so sorry, but he is in the villages and will not be back till night.' 'Praise God for that!' said the man, walking away with evident relief!

'Such a fellow deserves to be treated in the same way that he treats the nationals,' says a critic of the missionaries. 'How would he like to have a tooth extracted with no anaesthetic?' It does us all good to have a taste of our own medicine.

It happened during the second world war, when the Germans were patrolling the country. There was no petrol, cars were off the road and travelling was almost impossible. Abd alMasih developed severe toothache. A few days previously he had endeavoured to open an abscess on his own arm. He considered the tooth, a large molar. Could he extract his own tooth? He had succeeded with a root, but a molar? No, he would have to call in Lalla Jouhra. She had never extracted a tooth before, although he had had to operate on her. Now was her chance to get her own back! He gave her very detailed instructions. She put him on a chair in the corner where his head was held by the two walls and he could not escape. 'Now, apply the forceps, press them well down to get a grip of the roots of the tooth. Gently ease it from the socket and extract it,' he said to her. It sounded so easy, but there was no anaesthetic. She made an excellent job of that first extraction, but continued the slight rocking process longer than was absolutely necessary. 'Pull, pull,' he shouted. Out it came, and the only unprofessional touch was that the dentist, and not the patient, burst into a flood of tears. Doubtless, Abd alMasih showed far more sympathy with the next patient who came for tooth extraction – the European doctor!

One of the most effective weapons in spiritual warfare in Muslim lands is Christian love expressed in a practical way. Strange indeed that a man's respect and confidence can be won by extracting his tooth, or the appreciation of a woman by opening an abscess. Yet so it is. Suspicions are allayed, the love of Christ is seen in action, the bigoted spirit of a fanatical man is changed to a friendly receptive attitude. In hundreds of villages Abd alMasih was welcomed and his message received. The gospel was carried by patients over a very wide area, extending far into the Sahara desert. Yet never was Abd alMasih known as the *tebib*, or doctor. It was always 'sheikh' the teacher. While they appreciated the tender care and treatment, they understood even more the reason why he was there, to make Christ known. The most important consideration was that, amidst the crowds of self-satisfied Muslims who came for treatment, there were some timid souls who desired to know the Truth but who were deterred by the opposition and persecution meted out to all who openly accepted it. Such could quietly listen to the Scriptures under cover of the medical work. Some of these have undoubtedly been brought to know the Lord, and some of their stories will be told later.

Sick patients waiting

Chapter Eight

Discipleship – The Cost

Increasing opposition on every hand made Abd alMasih reflect that the Lord's servant is called in some measure to share in the sufferings of a rejected Lord. To a far greater extent must the converts face persecution and opposition. He often wondered that any were willing to stand against the fearful odds facing a Christian. He was amazed at the steadfast courage and perseverance with which men and women, boys and girls faced ostracism, blows and persecution for Christ's sake. To him it was one of the strongest proofs of the reality of the Christian faith.

Abd Allah seemed loth to leave the men's meeting although it was 10 p.m. The message had affected him deeply. He was obviously impressed, but he could not bring himself to decide for Christ. 'No,' he said, 'It's hard, too hard for me.'

'Surely you do not understand,' said Abd alMasih. 'To become a Christian is the easiest thing in the world. The Lord Jesus died on the Cross to save you, and you simply trust Him. He did it all. He finished the work for your salvation. You only have to accept Him.'

'Yes, I know. It is easy. IT IS EASY . . . for YOU, but it is HARD for US. So very hard,' he said.

What did this Muslim mean? He continued, 'Think of

all that I must face if I become a Christian. I am thirty-five years of age, and still live in my father's house. I work for him. As head of our house he sells the figs and oil and wheat and takes the money. With it he buys food for us all. We all live in one courtyard. We have our meals in common. If I do become a Christian he will disinherit me and turn me from his home. My wife comes from a very fanatical family, and she would at once leave me. I should have to bring up my four children alone. I could not remarry, because a Christian is permitted to have only one wife, and I could not divorce my present wife. I should be virtually alone and homeless and, even if I did find another room or house in which to live, I should be surrounded by Muslims. That means that I should be compelled to contribute to the support of the village sheikh who is of course a Muslim. When my daughters grow old enough to marry, no one would want to marry them. They would carry the stigma of being daughters of an infidel. If I sought employment elsewhere, no one would employ me in this Muslim land. When the men go to the mosque to pray, I could not join them if I were a Christian. In sickness and trouble they would not lift a finger to help me. In fact they would rejoice that I was under the curse of God and God was punishing me. Yousef is a Christian, and you know that when his baby died last year no one would help to bury it. Can you imagine his heartbreak? He had to dig the grave himself and bury his own child while the Muslims stood by and looked on, scoffing and jeering. That is what I dread most. The scoffs and the jeers. They would call me "an infidel dog". Every moment of the day I should show that I am a Christian, for I could no longer use the Muslim phrases that enter into every part of our lives. I could no longer swear, "By the truth of God", or "By the great Koran". I could not use any of the other oaths that my fellows employ every day of their lives. They would try and turn my mind with secret drugs and even attempt to poison me. My cousin is a shopkeeper and he would love to be a Christian, but then his shop would be boycotted. My children would suffer. Only last week I heard of Zouhra. She is only a child but everyone knows that she loves the Lord Jesus. Do you know that each week when she comes to your classes they throw stones at her as she comes along the street. Oh yes, Abd alMasih. It is easy . . . for you. But it is hard, so hard, for us.'

Ali was a regular attender. He was a working man with one child whom he loved dearly. How intently he listened to the Good News! To him it was as cold water to a thirsty soul. Others noticed his rapt attention, his sympathetic attitude, his serious manner. They decided that at any price he must be turned back. They told him that a good Muslim would not regularly attend gatherings at which the name of Mohammed was never mentioned. They reminded him that only a week or so before a man who attended these very meetings had been called from his home and shot dead. They were fully aware that this incident had had nothing to do with the men's meeting, but they could use it to discourage Ali. He replied, 'You can stop threatening me, for I shall never stop going to hear about the Lord Jesus. He loved me, and He loved me enough to die for me. I love Him dearly. In fact I would sooner die than turn aside from following Him.' They were bold words in a Muslim land.

Within a few days Ali was desperately ill and was taken to hospital. Although every effort was made to save his life, he died and went to be with Christ, which is far better, but he left a sorrowing widow and an orphan child. It was not until after his death that Lalla Jouhra was told by the women neighbours of the threats, of Ali's brave testimony and his determination never to turn aside. They knew, everyone knew, that Ali died as a Christian. It was sad to see his empty seat at the men's meetings. Numbers dwindled. The effect of his death on the work was disastrous.

So the opposition increased, but the servants of God plodded on.

One of the greatest tests for the Christian is the Fast of Ramadhan. Every Muslim is required to observe this, eating and drinking nothing from early morning until sunset for a month. The law of apostasy in Islam declares that whosoever breaks the Fast of Ramadhan is to be regarded as an apostate, whom to deprive of wealth or life is legitimate. A female apostate is to be confined in a separate apartment, starved and beaten daily until she returns to the faith of Islam.

In a Kabyle village the smoke rising from a small house proclaimed to all that the family in it was defying the law of Islam, the law of apostasy that is still valid in every Muslim land. More than this, it was known that the man and his wife were Christians. He was allowing his wife to prepare food during the day time, and they were both breaking the Fast. He had recently returned from France, where he had enjoyed liberty, but to cook food during Ramadhan in an Algerian village was an unforgivable offence. How dare they do such a thing? They must be taught a lesson . . . Two days later their delightful little babe was brought to the missionary, writhing in agony. Every effort to save the little life failed, and the lovely baby died. The next week the wife died, and the week after, the man. To this day Muslims curse and spit as they pass the graves. It is hard to be a Christian . . . in a Muslim land.

Various methods are employed to bring about death. One was discovered quite accidentally. An orphan girl, who had been adopted by missionaries, was afflicted with chronic enteritis. No treatment availed. Shortly before she died she passed a long hair in the faeces, and suspicions were aroused. Yes, it was foul play. Diligent enquiry elicited the following facts. Hairs are taken from a mule's tail and wound into a tight ball. This is encased in dough and forms a small pellet. The pellet is put into the couscous or *berkoukes*, which is swallowed without mastication. The dough dissolves in the intestine, the hairs unravel and provoke a chronic inflammation for which there is no cure. A qualified surgeon conducting a post-mortem would not easily detect the cause of death. Sometimes ground glass is mixed with the food and brings about a more painful death. In such cases it is not easy to trace the persons responsible.

While men meet with violent opposition, poisoning and death, a woman may have to face continual ostracism and persecution, and she has no one to whom she can turn. She is deprived of Christian fellowship.

Fathema was deeply exercised about her salvation. Her heart was touched to think that the Lord Jesus cared for her enough to die for her. She told her relatives, 'The Lord Jesus died for us all, not only for the Europeans.' At once everyone turned against her. They called her a *kafer*, a heathen. She no longer believed in Mohammed, but doubts remained in her mind. She could not forget the Word of God and, when Lalla Jouhra visited her, she used to look around furtively saying, 'Is anyone listening?' She drank in the message and wholly committed herself to Jesus her Lord. Then she felt that she could no longer pray as a Muslim, and told her husband so. 'Why not?' he asked. 'Because I am a Christian and Christians do not pray in that way.' He decided that it must be thrashed out of her, and whipped and beat her unmercifully. He threatened her with divorce. (To divorce her he had only to raise his hand

and say, 'You are divorced'. She would then have to leave the house and leave her children, go back to her father and be given again in marriage to a strange man. Her mother-heart yearned for her little ones.)

Then Ramadhan came round. Should a Christian, redeemed by the blood of Christ, observe the Fast? For His sake she ate and drank. Her husband came in and discovered her eating. Again he threatened her with divorce. As he sat in the coffee house drinking coffee, a near neighbour taunted him, 'Do you call yourself a man? You allow your wife to eat during Ramadhan? You have no moustaches, no pride.' One day he could stand it no longer. His pride was touched. He would show her and the neighbours who was master. He returned and beat her, compelling her to fast. (Her screams and sobs were evidence enough to the neighbours.) Now she was shunned even by her friends. They cleared their throats and spat at her whenever they passed her, or even when they passed her house. Her children were stoned and beaten because their mother was a hated Christian. She decided that she would continue to believe secretly in her heart. Nothing could change that. 'Why should I continue to suffer like this? I will be a Christian in my heart, but not let others know. God knows my heart,' she thought. She prayed. She fasted. Ramadhan was over but, to appease her husband, she fasted to make up for the days that she had missed. She paid the fine for not having fasted during Ramadhan. Her love for the Lord grew cold. She even told lies to shield herself, and that deep joy that she had when she first knew the Lord disappeared. Fear and shame turned her back. She is no longer a keen Christian, nor is she a Muslim. Yes, it is hard to be a Christian . . . in a Muslim land.

Waheeba wrote to her friend with whom she had been staying for a few days, 'You know well that I am a

Christian. The first thing that I did when I reached home was to pray and then I told my parents. I told them that I could no longer fast during Ramadhan. I explained why . . . and then all that evening, I assure you, I was hit on every hand. They all hit me. They said, "You will have to fast." I said, "I will fast, but I will not do it with intention. I will fast but with the intention in my heart to follow Jesus and not to obey Islam." They said, "You have betrayed your faith." Dear friend, I beg of you to help me for they want to marry me to a Muslim man. I am broken hearted, and I eat hardly anything. They told me, "We will throw you out." I said, "Yes, but even if you do, I will not deny my Saviour and renounce Him." Everyone is against me. I beg you to find me a shelter in a Christian family. My mother wants only the money she will get when I am sold in marriage to an old man. The younger the girl, the higher the price, and I am only fifteen.' What a choice for a girl only fifteen years old! To be put on the street for a life of shame or to be forcibly married to a Muslim man.

Basheer was the first boy whom Abd alMasih led to the Saviour, the first to be baptised, the first to suffer to the point of death, for Christ's sake. When first he attended the clinic, he sat among a crowd of men, clad in a ragged burnous which must have been handed down to him from several of his older brothers. His eyes were swollen and almost closed, and it was only with great pain and difficulty that he could lift his head and look at Abd alMasih. Carefully lifting the lids the latter found that the entire cornea of each eye was opaque, covered with a thin white skin. He had first seen the boy two days before in a wretched hut that Basheer called home. Heavy snow had fallen, and cow dung had been heaped on the fire in a vain attempt to warm the house. Basheer shivered in the cold. There was no chimney, and the smoke, which blackened the rafters and the walls, irritated his suffering eyes. It was quite evidently a case of neglected trachoma, which would ultimately lead to blindness. He was unable to go to the mosque to read or to attend school.

Nine years of suffering had passed since his birth, and now he had come to the clinic for treatment. Abd alMasih gave him some soothing eye lotion, and some mercurial ointment, telling him how to use them. As a result in five months there was a great improvement. He was able to attend the weekly class for boys.

Lalla Jouhra visited Basheer's mother every week. She was a Kabyle, and listened eagerly to the New Testament as it was read to her in her own tongue. There was no doubt about it. This message was for her. Cost what it might, she must give open expression to her faith. 'What has Mohammed done for us women? He has dragged us down, crushed us as grain in a mortar, and cowed and beaten us thus.' She illustrated her words by violently thumping her hand with her clenched fist.

'Since trusting the Lord Jesus, I have been blessed in every way. I have finished with all this superstition.' She took the charms from her neck and flung them into the open fire. Thus she made a clean break with the past. Fathema was a Christian.

It was a terrible thing in the eyes of Muslims for a high class Marabout woman like her to believe in Christ. Troubles soon began. Their only cow mysteriously died. Then one by one their goats died. Miriam the youngest daughter appeared to be possessed. She was demented, and finally died. Catastrophe after catastrophe fell on the family. Every one was a blow to Fathema. How much she looked forward to the weekly visits of Lalla Jouhra! Here at least was one in whom she could confide. Basheer now attended the class for boys. Although he could not read, he quickly learned some Scriptures by heart, and it was not long before he trusted the Saviour. The other members of the family were opposed. It was impossible for either Basheer or his mother to pray openly. Each night Basheer would creep into his mother's bed, and pulling the blanket over their heads, it became a little sanctuary. They prayed together in the precious name of the Lord Jesus. Fathema learned much from her son as he repeated to her the lessons he had heard in the classes.

One day when the men had gathered in the dispensary, and the meeting was in progress, Abd alMasih quoted two verses of the Bible that Basheer had learned, 'Christ died for our sins according to the Scripture, He was buried and He rose again, according to the Scriptures,' and 'The blood of Jesus Christ, His Son, cleanseth us from all sin.' The boy's voice rang out after the two texts, as he said, 'That is what I believe in my heart. I believe that Jesus died for me.' What looks of hatred were turned on him! '*Wa ma qatalu hu, wa ma salabu hu,*' repeated one. (They did not kill him, they did not crucify him.) 'I believe that He died for me,' said Basheer. But he was only a boy, and nearly blind, let his family deal with him. They let it pass.

For some months the weekly visits of Lalla Jouhra ceased. She and her husband had gone on furlough. Basheer and his mother were now alone. 'This is the time to frighten this fearless woman who claims to be a Christian,' thought the head man of the village. 'I will teach her a lesson that she will never forget, and openly expose her as a Christian.' She was a distant relative of his, bearing the same name, and at times he had access to her house. 'If you do not renounce your faith in Christ, and give some outward evidence that you are still a Muslim, I will disgrace you before all. Give us proof that you do believe in Mohammed. Pray, witness to Mohammed, buy some more charms containing verses of the Koran, and wear them, or else you will see what we do to an apostate

woman.' Fathema was terrified. To whom could she turn?
There was no one, no one except her Lord, and to Him she
poured out her heart.

Two days later an old woman came in. 'Muwatata, have
you heard the news? The head man is dead.' It seemed
almost incredible that that tall, strong man should have
been suddenly stricken down by God. 'Listen, you can
hear the wailing of the women. They are to bury him
today.' Could it be possible? The man who had threatened
to expose her, to illtreat her because she was a Christian,
and who was determined to make her recant, was dead!
She was safe! More than that, everyone would see that this
was the hand of God.

Fathema was more than ever convinced of the power of
the Lord Jesus. When Lalla Jouhra returned from furlough
Fathema said, 'I thought that you had left me for ever and
had forgotten me. But the Lord Jesus never left me. He
is with me here in this little hut. I am more than ever convinced that He alone is the Way.' What an encouragement
this was to Basheer! God had vindicated his mother's
faith. He decided that he too would follow – all the way.

The boys' classes continued and each week nearly
thirty boys attended. The Muslim sheikh listed the names
of all those attending the classes. At any cost this must be
stopped. Two sturdy young fellows were called to help
him. One by one the boys were taken to the mosque
by these bigger boys who roughly threw each one to
the ground. Were not these younger boys in danger of
becoming Christians? The boys' ankles were bound
tightly together, and the soles of their feet lifted in the air
by one big boy, while the other applied the *bastinado*. They
yelled, they screamed and struggled, but all in vain. Not
until twenty-five strokes had been well and truly applied
were they released. Then with swollen, blistered feet they
dragged themselves away. Basheer came in for a special

share of the torture. 'We will teach you to be Christians. It is strictly forbidden,' they said.

The next week Basheer came to the class surreptitiously, cautiously. Was anyone looking? He was so afraid. But he came . . . alone.

The years went by. Abd alMasih now lived at Lafayette and each Sunday morning there was a meeting there for Christians. It meant a long journey on foot for Basheer and his friend to attend, but Basheer was now a lad of fifteen and boys of that age are obliged to observe the fast of Ramadhan. His brother Belhaj knew well that Basheer would stay for dinner at the missionaries' home, even though it was Ramadhan. Why should he allow this young brother to dishonour the family continually? He would teach him a lesson that he would never forget.

Arming himself with a stick, Belhaj hid behind a rock, waiting for the two boys to come down the road. He was well away from the village, so that any screams would be unheard. He sprang out on them, and caught his brother. The stick fell on the weak boy's back with sickening thuds. 'Take that . . . and that. Remember . . . I will teach you to break the Fast, to disobey me.' Basheer fell to the ground unconscious, but Belhaj continued to rain blow after blow on his poor frail body. He regained consciousness and pleaded for mercy, but without avail. At last his brother's anger abated. He partly carried and partly drove the poor lad back to the village, driving him on with more blows. He dragged him to the mosque. There the sheikh added his quota of blows.

At last Basheer was released and dragged himself home. His mother spread the mat and made his bed, tenderly covering him with blankets. He was in the throes of fever. Pneumonia developed. His mother thought that he would die. She encouraged him, 'God still has work for you to do, my son. He will not let you die.' How his poor body ached! Where was his friend Abd alMasih? Why did he not come? Surely some one would tell him. But no one told him until ten days later. When he did see Basheer, the poor lad was covered from head to foot with bruises, his whole body was black and blue.

He recovered, but his constitution was shaken, and a little later that winter he was stricken with pneumonia. His mother asked Belhaj to go and tell the missionary and ask him to come but he refused. 'May God curse him and the religion of his forefathers! May He strike him blind! I would sooner see my brother die than go to a Christian for help!'

The following year Basheer decided that he would not provoke his brother by staying in the house during Ramadhan. He made his home in a little watchman's hut in the garden where he could watch the cucumbers. The rats were his only companions. He could nibble cucumbers and pomegranates, and thus break the Fast. Once more his brother found him and beat him. He then went thirty miles on foot to his mother's relations in Kabylia. There he stayed until the Fast had ended.

'It is the happiest day of my life!' said Basheer when he, a Marabout, was baptized. He was eighteen and at last, a man! What a victory it was for the Lord! 'At last I have been able to obey my Lord,' he said. Each Sunday he was present at the Lord's Supper and often engaged in worship.

Nine months later Abd alMasih was once more called to see him in his home. He was dismayed to see his emaciated form, his huge distended abdomen, to hear of the violent pains and uncontrollable dysenteric symptoms. He did his best to care for the poor lad. He had no car, for during the war there was no petrol and cars were off the road. There were very few medicines available. Every effort to save Basheer's life failed. He went to be with his

Lord, just nine months after his baptism. If any man follow
Me let him take up his cross. It is hard to be a Christian . . .
in a Muslim land.

'Take up thy cross and follow Christ,
Nor think till death to lay it down.
For only he who bears the cross
May hope to win the glorious crown.'

A persecutor

One of the persecuted

'Sifted as wheat'

Chapter Nine

This Woman Whom
Satan Has Bound

When a baby girl is born her arms are placed by her side, her feet are put together and then the whole body is wound round with dirty rags, leaving just the feet showing. The cradle is a very primitive affair, and swings from a beam in the roof. There are very few bed clothes, and the baby is effectively immobilised by the swaddling clothes. In this way she will spend the first months of her life, unable to throw off the blanket or to move about . . . Before a Muslim woman is buried her body is washed, after which sixteen yards of material are wound tightly round it. Thus the body is bound before burial. What an apt picture this is of a Muslim woman's life, bound from birth to death! We read in the Gospels of a woman whom Satan had bound for eighteen years, but who was liberated by the power of the Lord Jesus. The enemy of souls holds millions of Muslim women and girls captive by means of cruel customs which originated with, and are perpetuated by, Islam, and which blight and blast, degrade and debase their lives.

Careful observation over many years has confirmed the impression that in North Africa there are many women who are devout Christians. In their zeal and love for the Lord, their devotion to His Word and their deep desire to win others for Him, they often surpass the men, but Satan ensures that their sphere of influence and witness shall be strictly limited. They have found liberty in Christ, but the restrictions imposed on women by custom and cruelty ensure that their testimony is confined to one very small corner. This is one of the ways in which Satan works in Muslim lands.

'Come and see our little baby boy, sheikh. He is very ill and I am afraid that evil spirits have taken possession of him and made him blind.'

Baby had been born a day or two previously, after five days of suffering by the poor girl-mother. It was her first baby, and she was only a child herself. The birth had been protracted, so that Kabyle midwives had crowded round and used every possible means to effect a delivery. A heavy piece of wood had been rolled over the mother's abdomen to help expel the child. Now she was weak, and longed to be left to sleep, but she was not allowed to do so. She must keep her eyes fixed on her little son all day long for fear the evil spirits should take it away, and substitute a spirit child. Whenever she dozed off she was roughly shaken, and told to watch her child. She longed for a drink of water, but this was denied her lest the water should make her stomach swell. She was given oil and eggs to help her milk. The shrill cries of the women, and the continual clapping of hands made sleep impossible. As usual, there was great rejoicing because the baby was a boy. Guns were fired, and the women pierced the air with their '*you-yous*' and shouts of joy. Had it been a girl there would have been no such rejoicings. Baby is never washed but just smeared with oil, rubbed with salt and then wrapped in swaddling clothes. When the eyes swell and become inflamed it is attributed to the influence of evil spirits, and not to lack of cleanliness.

Some girls are allowed their freedom until they are fourteen years of age and in independent Algeria, an increasing number of girls are allowed to go to school, especially in the towns. At any time they may be shut away and this sometimes happens when they are only twelve years old. The deciding factor is not age, but physical development, and the reason is that immorality is rife. The punishment for immorality in a woman is death, especially if an unmarried girl becomes pregnant. She has brought dishonour on the family. When a girl is shut in, she is confined to her one-roomed house, and is no longer allowed to go out at will. Her studies come to an end. She may be permitted to go into the courtyard, but woe betide her if she is found peeping out into the road. If ever she is allowed out, she must be closely veiled and accompanied by a male relative or an old woman. Such a girl is occasionally allowed to go out to the public baths, to see a Doctor or, on very rare occasions, to go to a wedding. A young woman never goes for a walk, or does her own shopping. The man of the house brings in the food from the market, and her clothes from the local shops. More freedom is permitted to girls in the towns than in the country districts, and more restrictions are imposed on a better class girl than on a poorer lassie.

A girl may be given in marriage as early as twelve. She does not see her future husband before the wedding, and she has no choice in the matter at all. She must go to the man chosen for her by her father. He may be older than her father, and may possibly already have three other wives. She is then the man's darling for a short time, and is petted and spoiled, but she soon becomes, as the youngest wife, the drudge of the household. If a girl's father is absent from home, her uncle or older brother will sell her in marriage to the man he chooses. 'You may make of your wife anything that you like, except a corpse,' runs the proverb.

'Marriage is a kind of slavery in which man is the master,' wrote one of their learned, holy men. Child marriage is still common, though forbidden by law. It has the highest authority, for the prophet married Ayesha at the age of six, and they co-habited when she was only nine years old. She was his wife for nine years. Oh, the unspeakable sadness of the lives of many of these poor women and girls! In all fairness it must be said that in the towns conditions are rapidly improving. The girls are fighting for more liberty, and the abolition of the veil. Both fellows and girls are demanding to see their partners before marriage. The law of the land makes it illegal for a girl to be given in marriage under the age of sixteen, or without her consent, but such laws are often flouted. An increasing number of girls are going on to higher education, and some are completing their studies at Universities, but many a broken heart and thwarted life is to be found in the inland villages.

A young girl will often become successively the wife of four or five men before ultimately settling with her permanent husband. A woman may be divorced at any time at the whim of her husband. She has no choice, but has to leave everything that she possesses, including her children, and go back to her father. The man has simply to raise his hand and say, 'You are divorced,' and she must go. If he repeats the formula three times she cannot return to him until she has passed at least one night with another man. When divorced she must hand over her children to the care of another woman and never see them again. As often as not, the one who replaces her is a girl-wife, who could not care less for the babies and children of her predecessor. A married woman never takes the name of her husband, but retains her maiden name throughout life.

Abd alMasih sat with his host before a lovely bowl of couscous. On it had been placed a nice fat fowl. He had arrived in this village in time for them to prepare a meal for him. The lady of the house had carefully prepared the couscous and the soup. The chicken had been caught, quickly prepared and cooked. His host broke it into pieces with his hands, giving a leg and part of the breast to his guest and taking a similar portion for himself. The remainder was given to his sons who ate with him. His wife hovered round in the background. The meal finished, he called to her to take away the remains. She had to be content with what was left, and the neck and the claws. That was her portion.

Yet, *that chicken was the only thing that she had really possessed*, apart from her cheap jewellery. She had continually denied herself scraps of food to feed it, and the eggs that it laid were hers. She could sell them and use the money for herself, the only money that she ever had. But she was not asked to give the chicken. It was just taken . . . She had the neck and the claws. A trivial incident, yet it is the straw which shows how the current flows.

Nevertheless, it would be wrong to picture all Muslim women and girls as desperately unhappy. In fact the reverse is often the case, for they hide their sorrows. In country districts some women have much more liberty than those in towns. They can circulate freely in the courtyard of their homes. On market day, when all the men are away from the village, they can flit from house to house along the village street, or slip away to the fountain. The poorer women in Kabyle villages are sometimes allowed to go to work in the fields, or to gather olives. It is the woman who grinds corn, sifts the meal, and makes the bread or couscous. She takes the wool from the sheep's back, washes the fleece, spins it into yarn. Then she sets up the loom and makes the brightly coloured blankets, or the seamless burnous worn by the men. The blankets are wonderfully woven with beautiful, intricate designs.

Every part of a woman's life is linked with fertility and so the blankets depict the fields, the running water, the scales on the serpent's back. The imagery goes back to Eden, and the fertility of the fields is thought to be closely linked with that of the home. The blankets depict this in pictorial form. It is the woman who tends the animals, and milks the cows and goats. She plasters the walls of the houses within and without, and whitewashes them. She moulds the pottery and bakes it in the courtyard, at times covering it with artistic patterns. The men do all the sewing and embroidery, although an increasing number of women are getting sewing machines, and now make the dresses for the girls and women of their village.

Fear is always the controlling element in the life of a Muslim woman. She is always under the domination of a man. From early childhood her brothers are encouraged to beat her and illtreat her. When a child she is taught to fear the power of evil spirits, and talismans and charms are hung round her neck. When married she is subject to her husband, who compels her to carry out his every whim. The fear of divorce hangs over her head like the sword of Damocles. She fears the autocratic mother-in-law, for it is she who controls the household. When young the mother-in-law had been made to suffer, and she will see to it that her daughter-in-law suffers as much, or more, than she did. She tells her son about the defects and shortcomings of his wife, and encourages him to beat her. When there is a co-wife, each is afraid that the other woman will plot against her so that her husband will turn her out. She is afraid of the gossiping tongues of the old women who go from house to house and spread trouble, separating husband and wife. When her baby is born she fears the neighbours who will come in and covet it. A neighbour will enter the house and say, 'What a lovely baby!' She looks at the bairn with the evil eye. The poor baby soon refuses to eat, becomes sick, wizens and dies. They say that the demons have taken the true child and replaced it with a demon child. Above all, there is the fear of death and the hereafter, for many believe that women have no place in heaven. She shows this fear even in her devotions. It is fear that compels her to pray, to fast and to witness to Mohammed. She bows down to Allah and takes the abject attitude of a slave prostrating herself before a hard master. They know nothing of the love of God as shown in the Lord Jesus, that perfect love which casts out fear.

For the girls or women who do trust the Lord Jesus there is the same continual fear of evil tongues, of threatened divorce, of poisoning or drugs, of whippings or beatings, and of every form of ill treatment.

It is surprising how many of these women and girls love the Lord Jesus. They can usually be reached only in their homes, and it is tedious work, often involving hours of travel, to reach them. The stories of some of these women are given elsewhere in this book. Here is another.

Sameena is a girl of eighteen, a boarder at High School. When at school she is perfectly free to go about unveiled but, as soon as she returns to her village, she must put on her veil.

She lives in a house behind the blacksmith's shop owned by her father. She is never allowed out during the vacation. The only exit from the house is through the shop. Her father or brothers are always working there, and men bring their tools to be forged. She is virtually a prisoner, for no one can enter or leave the house without being seen by the men. Two years ago she trusted the Saviour, but she is never allowed to attend a meeting, or to have contact with those who could help her spiritually. She is limited to her Bible and her Lord. Once, before returning to school she was able to send a pencilled note to her missionary friend. It read, 'Please send me the Scripture Union Notes. I know so little, but I know Him, and that is what counts.' Imprisoned within the four walls of her home, bound by cruel custom, what can such a girl do to serve the Lord? Yet she has recently been a tremendous influence for good in the lives of two of her cousins, leading them to trust in the One she loves so earnestly and sincerely.

'This woman whom Satan has bound' so adequately describes the life of Muslim women. They are bound from birth to death, bound by cruel customs and superstition, bound by Islamic law, bound by man and by Satan. Only Christ can free them, giving spiritual liberty, yet many must spend their whole lives in physical bondage. Nevertheless, God is increasingly using the girls and women of Algeria to accomplish His plan.

Nothing is too hard for God.

So soon to be shut in

'Two women ... at the mill'

'Woman whom Satan hath bound'

Chapter Ten

Testings

To every servant of God there come times of testing. It would appear from the Bible that all such testings must be of an individual and personal character, as in Genesis 22. For this reason the record of the testing of Abd alMasih and Lalla Jouhra must be very personal. God never tests two individuals in exactly the same way, for no two characters are identical.

God had given them two fine children. Daisy was a lovely girl of nine years of age when the test came. She could speak French, Kabyle and Arabic quite fluently, as well as her native tongue. She had made excellent progress in her studies, had trusted the Lord Jesus for salvation and was a constant cheer and companion to her parents and to her younger brother. Yet she longed for the companionship of girls of her own age. The immorality of the local school made a French education impossible. A programme of lessons had been worked out so that mother and father took it in turns to teach the children without diminishing their service for the Lord.

The clouds of war hung ominously over Europe in September 1939. The whole family was on holiday at a seaside mission station, when a telegram arrived late one night intimating that some friends were due to leave for England in thirty-six hours. Would Daisy like to accompany them?

At five o'clock next morning her parents called her into their bedroom and put the position before her as clearly as they could. Would she rather stay with them in Algeria, or go to England? She chose the latter.

God alone knows the heart searchings, the deep sorrow, the bitter tears, the intense longing and the cost to all of that parting, and those long years of separation. When would they see her again? War was declared soon after her arrival in England. Later, France fell, all communications between North Africa and England were severed and when next they saw their treasure, she was a strapping girl of fourteen. After four and a half years of separation she hardly knew them, they scarcely knew her.

This trial of love must come sooner or later to all missionaries who have children. For Abd alMasih and Lalla Jouhra the choice was crystal clear. They could ignore the call of God, forsake the Lord's work, just at a time when they were mature missionaries and the work was developing, and return to England to care for their family. They could thus make a home for the children, enjoy their companionship, and the advantages of a civilised land with the privileges of Christian fellowship, OR, they could continue the work to which God had called them, the work for which the first years of their missionary life had prepared them, which would mean surrendering their dearest to the care of others during the most formative years of her life. This would mean in some ways exposing her to dangers and temptations, leaving her with no one to take the place of her mother. The situation was the more acute as her mother, herself the daughter of missionaries and separated from her parents for many years, knew all about the heartaches, the intense loneliness, the longings to be like other children who enjoyed their parents, the hundred and one little ways in which missionaries' children suffer.

Can the Word of God give us guidance under such circumstances? It definitely does.

1 The Lord calls for the supreme place in our hearts and affections. He declared, 'He that loveth son or daughter more than me is not worthy of me.' (Matthew 10:37).

2 The Lord is calling disciples who will stand by Him until the building of His church is complete, and the final victory over the powers of evil is attained. His conditions as seen in Luke 14:26–35 are therefore made plain.

3 The Father willingly sent His Son, the Darling of His heart, into a world where He was despised, and He experienced periods of utter loneliness. The Son of God willingly accepted the isolation, the suffering and the pain, in order that men should be saved.

4 The call of God is to a lifetime of service. While the sphere of service may widen as experience grows, and the character of our service may deepen as time passes, yet, the man who is called to Muslims will be faithful in reaching Muslims, the one who is called to Africa will labour faithfully in Africa until circumstances beyond his control indicate otherwise.

But every servant of God must make the decision for himself. Let there be no harsh judgement or unkind criticism of others who have been led to a contrary decision.

One tragedy of present-day missionary work is that so many couples leave their field of service after four years or more, never to return. Only rarely do the children of such parents become missionaries and, while the child of missionaries does not automatically become a missionary, it must be remembered that such are pre-eminently fitted for God's work. Such enjoy the unique advantage of ability to speak the language without accent, and above all the ability to adapt themselves, their lives and their messages to the mentality of the people.

The daughter they left for Christ's sake has for years been an honoured servant of God in Algeria, facing the challenge of the Muslim world.

When France fell in 1940, the Lord's servants in Algeria were cut off from all financial supplies emanating from England. Prices immediately soared, the shops emptied and it was virtually impossible to purchase clothing or medical supplies. Milk, butter, cheese, margarine and jam were unobtainable. Dates, oranges and charcoal, though products of the country, were sold at exorbitant prices.

In addition to this a baby girl was born to them, ten years after her brother. In normal times it was quite easy to trust God to supply the need, for a letter from England normally took only a few days. Can God spread a table in the wilderness? Who provides for the missionary in such circumstances? Is there anything too hard for God?

Years before, a Roman Catholic family had attended the gospel services for French people. Father, mother, daughter and granddaughter were deeply affected by the message, but made no open profession of conversion. They left the district and moved to the other side of the country. Abd alMasih and Lalla Jouhra had completely forgotten them. Out of the blue a letter arrived from them.

'Dear Friends, France has fallen. We understand that you are now cut off from all financial supplies from the United Kingdom. Please feel at liberty to draw on our account for as much money as you require, for as long a period as you need it. We cannot bear to think of a work such as yours suffering through lack of funds. We desire the work of propagating the Word of God to go on, and we want to help . . .'

Abd alMasih replied that they could not possibly avail themselves of this very generous offer, as it was one of their principles never to enter into debt, and they did not know when they could repay them. By return of post came a substantial money order, followed by another each month. God's work done in God's way can never lack God's supplies. There is nothing too hard for God.

In varying ways the need was supplied. A commercial traveller happened to be passing through, saw the need of medicines, and sent them a large consignment of the drugs his firm had in stock, the last they were to have for years. When the Jewish Doctor was compelled to relinquish his practice he passed on all his medicines. Kabyles would call in with a gift of oil, or figs. European farmers supplied them with wheat. Someone dropped a fleece of wool into the garden, so that it could be washed, spun into knitting wool, and used to knit the clothes which they so desperately needed during the cold weather. Apricot trees and vines, which had never borne fruit before, yielded bumper crops, enabling them to dry the fruit for use during the winter. The walnut tree produced ten times more than ever before. Ash leaves mixed with dried bramble leaves made excellent tea! In so many ways God provided.

When the new baby arrived the situation was most acute. They had literally come to the end of all supplies. The next morning there was a sharp knock at the front door. This was unusual so early in the morning and baby's arrival had meant a bad night. Not a person was to be seen, but there on the doorstep was a big hamper. In it was a large chicken, two and a half kilos of butter, four or five cheeses, four kilos of sugar, five kilos of excellent flour and some coffee. They had not had any of these things for months. Last, but not least, were some old sheets to be used to make nappies for baby. The missionaries wept for joy. How good is the God whom we serve! Whether in the matter of providing temporal supplies, or strength to go on, there is nothing too hard for God.

After the fall of France the Axis troops invaded Tunisia and hundreds of refugees fled from eastern Algeria. Later the whole of the country passed under the control of German and Italian Commissions. The enemies of the gospel seized on this opportunity and determined to bring the spiritual side of the work to a close. Abd alMasih was warned that all his movements were being watched by the *Sûreté*, or French Secret Police. Many French people were deeply affected by the fall of France and a series of weekly gatherings was organised for the study of the New Testament with a view to presenting the gospel message. These meetings were attended by the Judge and the Doctor, the two sub-Administrators, the wives of all the local policemen and by Jews, Protestants and Roman Catholics.

A well-conceived letter was sent to Vichy headquarters by the enemies of the gospel in which the missionaries were accused of political propaganda in favour of General de Gaulle, who was then in England. A list of over twenty names of persons attending the meetings was attached. Quite suddenly a substantial police force appeared in the little town. A detailed investigation was made in every house. The friends of the missionaries were very concerned. The wife of an official visited them and said, 'This is a very serious situation, and we are afraid that we shall all lose our places. There is no doubt that you will be interned, or even worse, and we wonder what will happen to your boy. We advise you to stop all spiritual work.'

What could they do? Cease all spiritual work? Continue some form of social work and omit all teaching of the Scriptures? Tone down their message? Abd alMasih decided to visit the Administrator.

'Sir, I wish you to be quite frank with me and to tell me what accusations have been brought against us.'

'I will be perfectly frank with you,' the Administrator replied, 'I can tell you nothing. However, if you go to the villages to preach the gospel, then preach the gospel. If you care for the sick people, and have an agreement with the Doctor then go on caring for the sick. If you have classes and meetings, then continue them. The visitation of the homes can go on. But there must be no political activity.'

How incredible! With feelings running so high, cut off from all supplies from the homeland, threatened with internment, surrounded by powerful political and religious antagonists and without legal aid, the missionaries had been told by this Administrator, a man of integrity and courage, to continue the work in every branch of their activities. The sequel is also almost as incredible – all the leading men of the town were removed, the Doctor lost his right to practise, the Administrator lost his place, his deputies were sent away, and the lonely servants of God, with no human aid, stayed on to continue God's work. Eventually all private cars except those running on methylated spirit were off the road, but the missionaries' car was still running with an S.P. (Service Publique) label and receiving a modest ration of petrol each month. It was a time of testing, but is there anything too hard for God?

With the fall of France and the occupation of North Africa by the Axis powers it seemed that all missionary work would be brought to a close. Some missionaries were interned, many were sent off to towns where they lived in *résidence surveillée* and were unable to contact the people. Stocks of essential foods and clothing were rapidly exhausted, and living conditions became increasingly difficult. There was no electricity, and the meagre allowance of paraffin did not keep lamps burning for long, so that even Europeans had to go to bed soon after sunset. Stocks of petrol came to an end, and the buses ran with a huge boiler at the back which was stoked with wood or charcoal. It was necessary to obtain permission to travel even a short distance. It seemed almost impossible to accomplish any effective work for God. Nevertheless, it was during these difficult years that a small assembly of Christians was formed and, until they left for England in 1943, Lalla Jouhra and Abd alMasih were able to continue their ministry, never at any time having less than fourteen meetings and classes each week.

The only way to reach Hammam was either to walk or to cycle. Abd alMasih bought a very old, decrepit cycle. The run downhill for six miles was delightful, even when he carried a large rucksack full of medicines on his back, but the long pull back in the noontide heat was very tiring. It was difficult to obtain any medical supplies and resort was made to herbs and plants. But the medical work continued and thousands still heard the message of life. Numbers grew in the classes until over one hundred and twenty children were attending the five weekly classes. The older girls learned to do knitting. It was impossible to buy wool in the shops, so fleeces of wool were purchased, the natural wool was spun and the girls learned how to knit. Then they returned home to make clothes for the family. There was a big class of tiny Arab girls. It was delightful to see them singing action choruses, and shutting their eyes tightly as the class closed in prayer. In the street they would run up to Lalla Jouhra so trustfully and catch hold of her hand, leading her to their homes where she was able to read the Bible to their mothers. Europeans dared not show friendship to the missionaries, and the trustfulness and love of the children was a cheer and comfort to them during the years when they were ostracised and despised because of their nationality. Forty homes were open to Lalla Jouhra, and she spent much of her spare time in making garments out of old clothes for the babies and small children. It was quite impossible to buy material, and wool was very dear. Many died of exposure and cold. Some families had one ragged garment only for the whole family. They would stay in bed under the one wretched blanket, and take it in turns to get a little exercise wearing the one garment. Others made a rough shirt out of a sack.

What a joy it was at such a time as this to see the nucleus of a small assembly! Basheer was now eighteen years of age and was baptised. He helped dig the baptistry in the hall, and said that he felt that he was digging a grave. He was dead and buried within nine months, but at his baptism he had declared, 'This is the happiest day of my life.' A Kabyle woman named Kakoo was also baptised. An old man named Zeetoonee was so weak that he could not be baptised, but in a remarkable way God delivered him from the bondage of Islam, and he came into fellowship with God's people. Tayeb and others also attended the gathering for Christians every Sunday morning. What joy it was to hear worship and praise ascending to the Lord from these erstwhile Muslim lips! It was worth all the sacrifice, to be able to maintain a testimony for God and to see Him working at such a time. From the commencement of the ministry the aim of the two servants of God had been, not merely the salvation of souls, but the formation of autonomous assemblies. Alas, the little assembly was short lived. Basheer was poisoned, Zeetoonee died and Ali was poisoned. Kakoo was the only one remaining, and after many years she fell into sin. Another knock-out blow! But they still went on.

With what amazement Lalla Jouhra and Abd alMasih listened to the announcement over the radio in September 1942 saying that British troops had landed on the North African coast. Throughout those long dark years of war, when almost all postal communications with the United Kingdom had been severed, they had carefully locked the outside gate each evening and had placed heavy blankets over the windows. Then they had tuned in to London, turned the wireless set down to a mere whisper, and listened to the news. It reminded them constantly of the Christian's need to listen in! He, too, lives in enemy territory, and is surrounded by lies. He can continue in effective service only as he listens through the Word to the living Voice of the One who is sure to triumph.

Long convoys of troops were now travelling on the main roads, but Lafayette was far from the beaten track. Abd alMasih felt that he must see for himself. He mounted the decrepit old cycle and rode for twenty-five miles to the main road. The military must have thought that this lone man who stood by the roadside cheering was completely out of his mind. They never imagined that he was English, and of course the convoy could not halt.

Their little son had suffered during the preceding years. He had been stoned and insulted whenever he went outside. Now he was a hero, riding round with the soldiers and acting as interpreter. The only shoes that could be bought were those made from old motor tyres. He had on trousers made from his mother's old skirt. His coat was made from a blanket that had been dyed, and his pullover and socks had been knitted from natural sheep's wool. Wandering up to a mechanic working on a plane, he was told to clear off. Straightening himself up, he said 'I'm English, sir.' The man pushed his hat to the back of his head and exclaimed, 'Blimey, where did you drop from?' Whereupon John had to ask mother what that word meant. The soldiers spoilt him quite a bit. Returning one day he was violently sick.

'What have you eaten, boy?'

'For dinner I had a tin of sardines, two packets of chocolate, some bully beef, biscuits and lots of things besides.'

'But you did not eat a whole tin of sardines?'

'They kept on saying to me, "Go on John, don't be afraid." So I did.' He was ten years old, and it was essential that he should go to school. The baby was suffering from malnutrition and lack of vitamins, so that her little finger nails were turning black and dropping off. It was essential to get away as soon as possible.

At the end of June Abd alMasih and Lalla Jouhra with the little family embarked at Algiers on a former Dutch liner for the United Kingdom. The usual four-day journey took them well over a month. What a journey it was!

How thankful they were for the protecting hand of God during that voyage with small children! They arrived safely in the United Kingdom: land of comparative plenty. Everywhere people were complaining of their small rations, but to be able to eat butter and cheese, margarine and jam once again was wonderful. And to have clothing coupons which one could use seemed too good to be true!

Chapter Eleven

Back to the Battlefront

Once more Abd alMasih was faced with a difficult choice. On Armistice Day in May 1945 very serious riots broke out at Setif, and these extended to Lafayette and Lesser Kabylia. Over one hundred Europeans were cruelly massacred by the Muslims, and the army retaliated by murdering thousands of nationals. It created an atmosphere of bitterness and hatred which was not conducive to mission work. Only the timely action of a French army officer had saved the whole European population from being massacred.

The authorities refused to allow Lalla Jouhra to return with her husband to Algeria. Abd alMasih again had to choose between remaining in England with his wife and three children, or returning alone to the work to which God had called him, and from which he had been unavoidably absent for just over a year. He returned alone to a land of famine. Snow had fallen to a depth of over three feet on the High Plateaux during the month of January. Day after day it fell for a whole month. Roads were blocked. The weight of snow pressed down on the surface of the ground, and rendered it hard. The snow melted in two days, and then the pitiless sun beat down month after month. There was no rain. The surface of the ground was baked hard. Very little of the sown wheat and barley germinated. Then hordes of locusts devoured everything green and also the corn. Riots followed, and for weeks people were afraid of leaving their homes for fear of being killed. The result was famine. Everywhere were the carcases of animals that had died of hunger. The Americans had sent stocks of wheat, but this served to provide only one small meal a day. Soon these stocks were exhausted, and during that winter many a family subsisted for three months or more on the roots of wild arum and other mountain plants.

Some men managed to keep a bushel or two of wheat for sowing. These men were faced with a hard choice. They could sow this corn or use it to feed their families. It could be sown or eaten, one thing or the other. There was not enough to do both. A man could quite literally take the children's bread and sow it, casting it on the surface of the soil, ploughing it in, hoping for a harvest. It certainly needed much courage and considerable faith to take the food from the children, send them to bed hungry and then deliberately sow that corn. To some people it seemed so utterly unreasonable, so illogical, even cruel; but a moment's reflection showed that if there was to be a harvest the choice was inevitable.

As Abd alMasih meditated on the sacrifice made by these men in order to secure a harvest, he realised that he too had been called to sow in another realm. He had come to sow the Word of God in the hearts of these people. Some Christians had criticised him for leaving wife and family to sow the Word. They had not failed to point out that there had been no spiritual harvest in North Africa and that there never would be. But God was teaching him another lesson – He himself must be sown. Now that he was alone among these tens of thousands of men and women, in an atmosphere of bitterness, hatred and suspicion, he realised to the full his nothingness, his smallness, his aloneness. In returning to Algeria alone, at such a time, he was surely throwing away his life. Yet what had his Lord said? 'Unless a grain of wheat falls into the earth and dies, it remains alone; but if it dies, it bears much fruit.' 'He who loves his life loses it, and he who hates his life in this world will keep it for eternal life. If any one serves me, he must follow me; and where I am, there shall my servant be also'(John 12:24–26 RSV). He knew that the Lord Jesus was like that corn of wheat. He died that we might live. Through His death we have life, eternal life.

Was there not here a deeper, profounder truth? The Lord was calling His disciples to follow Him, to become grains of wheat, to die to self that their lives might be fruitful. Abd alMasih realised that God was calling him to do just this. Many years before he had had to choose between the self life and a life of service. But the choice must be faced again. It faced him at every step. He could still return to his dear ones, to the comforts of the homeland; or he could face the hardship, the lack of food, the loneliness and throw away his life in these villages. He shrank from the loneliness. But the words re-echoed in his mind and heart, 'If any one serves me, let him follow me.' Yes, he wanted to serve the Lord, he wanted to see a harvest of souls. Then he must follow his Lord.

Where was the Lord Jesus when He spoke these words? He was going to the Cross. His pure and holy soul shrank from the suffering. 'Father, what shall I say? Save me from this hour? No, for this purpose I have come to this hour.' The Saviour had gone on, like the grain of wheat under the sod, swelling, suffering, bursting, dying, yet bringing forth new life. He had died, He had been buried and had risen again, and at Pentecost there had been a glorious harvest of souls. Now He was calling His servant to follow Him.

Seed corn can be eaten or sown. If it is eaten it produces

no fruit. This is the first lesson that the Lord would teach His servants. We must fix our eyes on Him. He is worthy of our sacrificial service, our loyal devotion, our utmost love. Reader, will you hold a grain of wheat in your hand? Look well at it. It represents your life. How small, how insignificant it is! But you can never really see a grain of wheat by holding it in your hand. To see it with its vast potentialities it must be thrown away. It must be sown. So with your life. This choice comes to every one of us repeatedly. Perhaps the reason that there is so little harvest today is that Christians live too much for self. My life can be spent for self or it can be given in sacrificial service. Which shall it be?

In our day and age it is possible for the average young man to attain proficiency in the subject of his choice. It should be the aim of every potential missionary to graduate, to attain a diploma or a degree before proceeding abroad in the Lord's service. In former years financial considerations often debarred a man from a university education, but this is not so today. The graduate in Science or Art and the nurse with her SRN have their whole lives before them. How shall these lives be spent? Surely these years of training should not be deliberately thrown away and sacrificed? Yet that is the sacrifice that the Lord demands. The medical graduate who goes out to face the disease, poverty, dangers, suffering and isolation of Africa appears to throw away his life. He buries himself in a foreign land as a grain of wheat. Yet the Lord says that such a man, the man who hates his life in this world, is the only man who keeps it. The man or woman who hangs on to his own life, to worldly prospects, and seeks financial gain appears to have found his life, but in reality he has lost it. Let us each be prepared to yield our lives to Him in sacrificial service in the place of His choice, be it at home or abroad. This then is the first step in a pathway of sacrificial service.

Abd alMasih went to the market. Thousands of men had gathered, the men he had come back to reach. But how? Again he felt his nothingness, his utter helplessness, that acute awareness that he was alone; if only there had been a team of workers!

Once more his thoughts turned to the Word of God. Among those teeming masses of men were some the Lord Jesus called, 'My sheep.' Abd alMasih did not know who, but the Lord said, 'I know them and they follow Me.' How could he reach such men? How could he know them? 'If any one serves Me, he must follow Me, and where I am there shall My servant be also.' The verse rang in his mind. The Lord Jesus would lead him to those men. They were His sheep. He knew them. He had been surprised to learn that one possible connotation of the word follow, is 'to trudge through the dust.' It conjured up a picture of the eastern servant trudging through the dust at the feet of the master's camel, following his master. His thoughts turned to Philip. He had been engaged in a very successful ministry at Samaria. Then it was that the angel of the Lord spoke to him saying, 'Arise and go toward the south, unto the way that goeth down from Jerusalem to Gaza, which is desert!' Philip had obeyed, and there in the desert he had seen the dust arising. There could have been no more unlikely place for an evangelist to work in than the great desert. In that chariot was a seeking soul. But surely His Master was there too. The Ethiopian was seeking the Saviour, just as sincerely as were the Greeks in John 12. The eunuch had the Word of God. The Lord was preparing his heart, creating a deep yearning, a longing to know Him. He was one of those other sheep. The human servant was needed.

The Lord led His servant. The servant was in close communion with his Lord, and the vital contact was established between the sinner and the Saviour. One of those 'other sheep' heard the Shepherd's voice. Thus it is that the Lord works in fulfilment of the principle, 'where I am, there shall My servant be also'. Where He is working, creating a sense of need, there should His servant be, to encourage, to point the way and to speak of Him.

This is the acme of successful service. Yet how often we fail. We are not close enough to the Lord to hear His voice and the opportunity passes, never to return. Thus the Lord will not lead only to the sphere of service, but to the very persons we are to contact. The principle is seen at work throughout the great missionary book of the Acts. The Lord led Ananias to Saul of Tarsus. He established contact between Peter and Cornelius. He led Paul to Lydia, to a jailor, to Aquila and Priscilla. In each of the three missionary journeys He led to fresh towns and to the persons of His choice. Oh, the thrill of experiencing such leading! This principle is as true in Africa as in the United Kingdom.

How lonely must Philip have been in the desert! How futile seemed that long journey! Now Abd alMasih was feeling lonely, realising the futility of his long journey back to Africa. He had come to seek those who were apparently utterly unconcerned about their souls. He was seeking those 'other sheep'. How could he find them? His prayer was, 'Lord lead me to some seeking soul; to one of those sheep.' He had not long to wait to see that the principle really worked.

A number of men and boys had gathered round Abd alMasih and were listening well to the story of the prodigal son. Suddenly the village sheikh appeared. He was a red-bearded gentleman with a very violent temper. Striking right and left with his thick stick he scattered the boys and ordered the men to leave. Having dispersed the audience he retired to the mosque to pray. When the men and boys came back to listen the Muslim leader returned to the fray with renewed zeal. His heavy cudgel fell with sickening thuds on the backs of the boys. They all turned and fled before his fury. Snatching the chart of 'The Two Ways' he flung it to the winds, and did the same with the New Testament that Abd alMasih was holding. Raising his thick stick over the head of the missionary he cursed him, calling him 'Christian dog', and demanded why he had dared to return to this village when he had been ordered not to do so. It was useless to seek to continue under such circumstances, and there was no alternative for Abd alMasih but to leave with a heavy heart, and with the curses and threats of the sheikh ringing in his ears. The village chief followed him to the outskirts of the village and said, 'He has an awful temper, but in three months' time his term of office will be finished. We shall sack him and send him back to his village. After that you can return to us whenever you like.'

The following year Abd alMasih remembered the invitation to return to that village, and had a most encouraging time in the tribe. Towards evening, when he was wending his way over the mountains back to his car after a long and tiring day, he heard a voice shouting to him, 'Oh sheikh, stop. Wait for me!' He had started the day at 4 a.m. and had been tramping over the mountains for twelve hours. He had spoken to groups of men in five villages and was both mentally and physically tired out. Looking over his shoulder he spotted a religious teacher hastening to overtake him. He quickly recognised him as the brother of the red-bearded gentleman with the violent temper, the man who had so persistently opposed the message the previous year. Abd alMasih hastened his step. He was too tired to enter into controversy, and was anxious to get home. The Muslim was so determined to reach Abd alMasih that he actually condescended to run. 'Stop!

Stop!' he shouted. He soon overtook him. 'How is it that you visit every other village in Kabylia but ours?' were his opening words. 'You never come to us and there are those in our village who need your message, they want to hear.'

Abd alMasih replied, 'On two occasions I have visited your village, but not a single soul has troubled to come to the mosque to listen. Also you must remember that some of your own family do not want me to preach the gospel. They are afraid that if Kabyles follow the Lord Jesus, they will no longer need Muslim teachers. I myself have very strong proof that some of your family are opposed.'

'Come to our village as soon as you can,' was the earnest request, 'Some people there really need you.'

At the earliest opportunity, although with certain misgivings, Abd alMasih tramped across to the village and climbed up to that quarter where the Marabouts, or religious leaders lived. There was no sign of his Marabout friend. He had left the previous week to go to live in a distant town. Abd alMasih therefore went to the other quarter of the village where the Kabyles lived. A number had gathered and were sitting on a large rock waiting for him. They welcomed him cordially and encouraged him to speak to them. He had not proceeded very far with his message when there was an interruption from a man called Ali.

'Tell me, teacher, what must I do to have forgiveness for my sins?'

The Holy Spirit was at work. Very simply Abd alMasih outlined the work of the Lord Jesus. 'Without the shedding of blood there is no forgiveness.' 'This is my blood which is shed for many for the forgiveness of sins.' 'Whosoever believeth on Him shall receive forgiveness of sins.' Ali repeated the words from the Bible as they were read.

'Can I have forgiveness now?'

'Yes, if you will believe in the Lord Jesus.'

The meeting over, the servant of God left, but the awakened man followed him to the outskirts of the village. Said he,

'Tell me again what I must do. Do you mean that I must repent and turn from all my efforts and simply trust in the Lord Jesus?'

Ali trusted the Saviour that day. There is no doubt about the sincerity of his faith and love for the Lord. Every fortnight Abd alMasih visited him in his village. He went from strength to strength and taught himself to read the Bible. Through his witness five or six others trusted the Saviour. It was the first time that a group of Christians was gathered in a Kabyle village. It was almost a local assembly. The Lord clearly led His servant to that isolated village, the village which he had so studiously avoided. He used most unusual means, making the wrath of man to praise Him, showing clearly that He is Lord of all and will ultimately gather all those other sheep until there is one flock, one Shepherd.

Chapter Twelve

His Own

The fact that they are His sheep, reminds us not only of His Shepherd care, but of their weakness and dependence on Him. He sends them out as sheep in the midst of wolves. He speaks of their enemies as thieves and robbers, strangers and hirelings. It is evident that the search for these sheep will involve a struggle. This and the following chapters tell something of this.

Back again in Algeria Lalla Jouhra resumed her visits to the women. She had just left the house to visit some of the shut-in ones when a young boy ran up and said, 'My mother and sisters want you to go and teach them God's Word.' He gave the name of a shopkeeper in the main street of the village. She found the courtyard and was given a warm welcome by the mother and the two girls. From the first the gospel message gripped them and it was always a joy to visit them. Not one of them was ever allowed to go out of the house, as they were from a Marabout family. The name of the elder daughter was Joy. She had lived for some time with her French aunt who was a schoolteacher. This woman had married a Kabyle, by whom she had twin boys; Joy cared for them while her aunt taught in school. The comparative freedom of a French home meant that Joy became rather too friendly with quite a number of village fellows. Her father heard gossip about her and soon sold her in marriage. It proved a very unhappy union, and Joy was soon divorced and back with her mother again. While living with her aunt she had learned to read and write, and she was quite a clever dressmaker. She was also an artist and drew her own designs for her embroidery. Life was very limited in that dark damp yard, with its high surrounding wall; the two small rooms in which they lived were so dark and hot. However, during the late afternoon the sun reached the attic. Joy often climbed the ladder to the attic to get a little sunshine and air.

Then Joy was married again, this time into a fanatical family that was most opposed to the gospel. How would it be possible to reach her there? She had taught herself to read in Kabyle, her own language, and she loved to meditate in the four Gospels. Lalla Jouhra visited the bride in her new home, a small rented room in the relatives' courtyard. The boys of the household were very opposed. At each visit they stood outside, jeering and laughing, making fun of the Lord's Name. Joy did not hide her light and had the Word of God with her, so that when the neighbours came in she could read to them. Shortly after, she and her husband moved back to her father's home. There they lived together in the little attic at the top of the ladder. One corner was curtained off as a bedroom, with the mattress on the floor. The other part had a small piece of lino on the floor to exclude the draughts from below. There was a small round table and two stools and cooking was done in a couple of saucepans on a primus. What a little sanctuary that attic became as Lalla Jouhra and Joy studied the book of Acts together, the mother and sister listening below! Joy had learned some hymns, which they sang together, and each session ended with prayer. Joy soon saw her need of accepting the Lord as her personal

Saviour. How thrilled she was to learn about a baptism!
One day she said, 'I, too, must be baptised, now that I
believe in the Lord Jesus.'

One day her husband quarrelled with his mother-in-
law and they went to live in a damp, dark room which was
really a passageway leading into a courtyard full of
women. It had previously been used to store wood. One
door gave out on to the street and the other door on to the
common courtyard. Water dripped from the iron girders
of the roof and soaked into their bed. It was so dark that it
was impossible to read without a light. This was where
poor Joy spent her life. She was too ladylike to mix much
with the rough women in their courtyard and to share
their coarse jokes.

In the door was a little keyhole, and through this she
used to watch for Lalla Jouhra to come on the afternoon
that she visited her. She also read the Scriptures with her
husband when he returned from his work. There were
often dark looks from the neighbours as the missionary
passed and greeted them, and when she left the house the
boys would often throw stones at her. The Muslims deeply
resented her visits and were most opposed.

One afternoon Joy's uncle came in. He was the fanatical
sheikh with a red beard who had so opposed Abd alMasih
in the villages. He found Joy following a correspondence
course, with the book open on the table with her Bible.
While she made a cup of coffee for him, he asked for a box
of matches. She quite thought that he wanted to smoke,
but smelling something burning, she turned from her little
stove with a cry of dismay. He had piled her books on the
cement floor and was burning them. Then he turned to her
and cursed her for daring to read such books. How frightened she was as she recounted the incident to Lalla Jouhra
on her next visit! A day or two later her husband visited
the missionary. His head was swollen and his face

blackened with bruises. During the preceding night their front door had been broken down and a gang of roughs had beaten him up. He asked Lalla Jouhra not to visit Joy again until they had been able to move to another district. How she missed her weekly visits to Joy, but how much sadder for the poor lonely girl in the dark, damp room! She had no friends to share her trouble, her precious Bible had been destroyed and there was no weekly visit to anticipate. She was shut up to fellowship with her Lord.

After an absence of several years Lalla Jouhra returned to Algeria for a visit and was staying in an apartment in Algiers. She had been able to get Joy's address and wrote to her inviting her to come with her husband. It was deemed wiser for them to come to her than for her to visit them. The following evening the doorbell rang and there stood Joy and her husband. Their joy was unbounded, her face was a picture. Her husband turned to her and said, 'At last we have found Lalla Jouhra. Since coming to this great town I have so often looked into the faces of the women to try and see her. I knew that she was somewhere in this vast city.' They had a happy time of fellowship together.

A few days later the Scriptures in Kabyle were sent to them again, but alas, they had once more changed houses and the parcel never reached them. Muslims watch professing Christians very closely and it may well be that this fleeting contact with missionaries had been discovered. Even letters are intercepted, and everything possible is done to make the Christian shut-in women feel their isolation, so that they grow discouraged and turn from the Lord. What a joy that short contact brought to Lalla Jouhra and to those lonely Christians! To see their radiant faces, to know that their hearts had not changed, to hear their deep desire to know more of the Lord was balm to her spirit. But now they are lost in the crowds of that great Muslim city. Lalla Jouhra can only bring them daily to the Lord in prayer, asking that He will complete the work that He has begun in their hearts. The missionaries have left but the spiritual struggle continues. The sheep are in the midst of wolves, but there is nothing too hard for God.

'Oh! Lalla Jouhra, look at my beautiful new boots. They are for me to wear when I go to the mosque to learn to recite the Koran.' Rashid was so proud of his boots, but the missionary was saddened to think of him reading the Koran for his father had been regularly to the classes. He was a Kabyle lad, and at the mosque learned chapter after chapter of the Koran, repeating from memory the Arabic words that the sheikh had written on the wooden slate. What matter that he understood very little of the passage he recited? A boy's memory must be trained to the utmost, but he is not taught to reason or think. On Thursday Rashid was at the boys' class, proudly displaying those new boots. Sundays and Thursdays are school holidays and these are the days chosen for classes for junior and senior boys and girls. On Thursday the Muslim sheikh had a holiday, so that Rashid was free to attend the Christian class. He was limping badly and Abd alMasih examined his hip. There was little doubt that he had T.B. He was advised to consult the local Doctor who said there was little that he could do for him. It was not long before the heart of this boy opened to receive the Saviour. He asked if he could come to the meeting for Christians on Sundays, and it was there that he learned to sing the Kabyle hymns that he loved so well.

He was able to attend school and being bright and intelligent he quickly learned to read in French. His school days were short-lived, however, for his back was so painful that he could only hobble around the garden. He longed to be with other Christians, so each Sunday morning Abd alMasih got out his car, and went down to bring the poor helpless cripple to the gathering. What music it was to hear him pray! It was evident that he sincerely loved the Lord.

The pain in his back increased and soon an abscess burst, so that he had to spend most of his time in bed. It was then that he asked for the New Testament in Kabyle, which he soon learned to read. When the missionary visited him on one occasion Rashid said, 'I try to explain to these women about the Lord Jesus, and to show them how they can be saved, but they seem to be blind and cannot see it.' 'These women' were his grandmother and his mother, some of his nieces and aunts! Every morning he would call them to come while he taught them to sing and read to them a passage of Scripture. 'A little child shall lead them.' Lalla Jouhra used to visit them too, and Rashid would listen intently to the message.

The months slipped into years, and Rashid suffered intensely. The only cure would have been to immobilise the whole vertebral column by putting him in plaster for a year, but his parents refused to allow him to enter hospital. He suffered acutely from one abscess after another which formed in his hip and back. Then, for a few weeks, he recovered sufficiently to hobble round the garden and to attend the Christian meeting again. How his face shone with the joy of the Lord!

A boy of his age in England heard about him and wrote to him, sending a French Bible. How proud he was of his Bible bag, which now contained a Bible in French, a New Testament in Kabyle and a hymn book, as well as a clockwork motor car! The bag was hung on a nail, well out of the way of the other children, but he could never run that precious motor himself, he was too ill.

It was evident that the end was not far off. One evening both Lalla Jouhra and Abd alMasih went to see Rashid. His whole body had been terribly swollen and bloated, but now the swelling had gone and it seemed that his poor emaciated frame was covered only with skin. Every bone could be seen. He smiled sweetly when they went in and prayed with him. When they returned from Kabylia the next day, the parents asked them to go down again. It was late at night, and they read to Rashid, 'The Lord Jesus Christ shall change this body of humiliation that it may be fashioned like unto His glorious body.' 'When we see Him, we shall be like Him.' Death held no terrors for Rashid, he was going to meet his Lord. They glanced back as they reached the door, and for the last time saw his lovely, wistful smile. It was 'Goodbye'. Before morning Rashid had passed into the immediate presence of the Lord he loved so dearly, his pain and suffering over.

His family dared not bury him as a Muslim; they knew he was not. Political conditions made an open Christian burial impossible. Four 'old boys', men who had attended the Christian classes, carried him away to the cemetery. There was no Muslim sheikh, no plaintive chanting and wailing. Only his relatives and friends followed him to the grave. Lalla Jouhra and Abd alMasih stood in silence as they carried that frail shell past the house to its last resting place. 'My sheep hear my voice, and I know them, and they follow me and I give them eternal life.'

Ali sat up on his bed and coughed. It was only with great effort that he was able to express his gratitude. He said,

'Thank God you came and told me about Him before I die! We did not know that the glory of the Lord Jesus far surpasses that of Mohammed. No one had ever told us that Jesus died for us. We did not know that God forgives our sins when we trust the Lord Jesus. We thought that we could hope only for forgiveness after years of fasting and prayers. Thank God you came and told me about Him!'

It had been an effort for Abd alMasih to visit Ali. The

melting snow on the mountains had swollen the stream in the deep ravine until it was an angry, swirling torrent. The servant of God had seen the black clouds and the threatening storm before he left the shelter of the car. He had been sorely tempted to continue his way home without attempting to visit that lonely child of God. In vain he looked for some means of crossing the torrent at the usual ford. He went upstream for a mile in the teeming rain, then plunged knee deep into the icy water, and climbed up to a height of 3,000 feet. The rain turned to snow, and he fought his way through the blinding snowstorm to arrive at last at the house of his friend and brother in Christ. Now he sat in the smoke of the house, sipping a cup of black coffee and eating a few figs with some dry Kabyle bread. Ali's wife was no cook, but he had to make pretence at enjoying the coffee, which tasted rather of paraffin, and the hard smoked bread. He was chilled to the bone, but how heartwarming to hear those words from the sick man! 'Thank God you came and told me before I die!'

Ali was suffering from acute T.B. of the lungs. During the second world war he had been trapped in Belgium, evacuated from Dunkirk, then sent back to France and eventually repatriated. He had been nursed by a Roman Catholic sister who had spoken to him of Jesus Christ and His atoning death, but there was much that he could not understand until Abd alMasih had visited his village and he had believed in the Lord Jesus. He had a pension from the French army and a liberal allowance for his wife and two children, so that he was independent. Most Muslim men of his age are dependent on their fathers. They share everything with their adult brothers, and are often unable to break with Islam because of family ties. Ali was free to follow the Lord. Having heard the gospel and having believed, he was determined by the grace of God to become a true disciple. Using the Laubach method he

soon taught himself to read in Kabyle. 'Each one teach
one' was the motto, so that he was anxious to pay his debt
and teach someone else to read. He found several apt
pupils. All went well until one day he was asked,

'Ali, if we learn to read in Kabyle, what can we read?'

'The New Testament in Kabyle, of course,' he replied.

'But surely there are other books?'

'I will ask sheikh Abd alMasih,' he said

'Can I read the newspaper in Kabyle?'

'No, but there is God's Word, that is to be preferred to
any newspaper.'

'Then we are to understand that you want us to read the
New Testament and to become Christians. Perhaps you,
too, are a Christian?'

'Yes, I believe that the Lord Jesus died for me.'

The reading lesson had ended in uproar. They had
turned on Ali with bitter words, cursing him, spitting at
him and telling him that he knew nothing. They brought
along the village sheikh who did all in his power to over-
throw the faith of this determined man. It was useless. Ali
knew that his sins were forgiven. The news spread. From
near and far men came to speak with him, to find what
was the reason for his assurance. One learned man
brought his Koran with him. After talking with Ali, he
pointed to the Koran and said,

'There is no forgiveness in this book. I have read it from
cover to cover, and it has no message for me.' How avidly
he listened as the Christian told him of the Son of Man
who has power on earth to forgive sins.

The Muslim *ulama* (doctors) were deeply concerned.
This determined witness to Christ must cease. He must
either be brought back to the fold of Islam or be killed, but
how? Ali had to report at hospital every three years for a
check-up. Failure to report at the appointed time would
result in the loss of his pension. Here then was the way to

force this despised Christian to return to Islam or to break him, to intimidate him and to kill him. The village postman destroyed the first letter which fixed the date of the hospital appointment, then the second and finally the third. Meanwhile Ali waited for the letter that never came. At last he decided to take the long journey to Constantine, by donkey, bus and train.

The advice offered at the hospital was,

'Go back to your home and wait. We will inform you when a hospital bed is available. Then return here at once.'

Ali returned to his mountain village but no letter from the hospital ever reached him. The Muslims made quite sure that it should not. He lost his pension. He was penniless and needed medicine, wood to heat his home, food for his family. Abd alMasih persuaded him to accept a gift of five pounds, but he would take no more. His courage was undaunted. Every evening he gathered his family for prayer. He read to them from the New Testament. Peacock, his wife, professed to believe, his lovely young daughter trusted the Saviour and his elder brother did so, too. It was evident that God was working in this village.

Ali himself was extremely keen. To Abd alMasih he said, 'Sheikh, can you not arrange a special effort to tell the whole village. Bring over a film strip. That will help the men to understand.' The car battery was disconnected, loaded on to a donkey with the projector and a screen set up on the big rock where the men gathered. Darkness fell, and even the youngest, prettiest woman, who was shut away, could creep out and peep over the wall at the pictures. 'To seek and to save' was the subject, and they could all understand that three-fold parable of Luke 15. How thrilled Ali was to be able to witness to his Lord! His brother's wife, a little hunchback, and his nephew professed to believe. There was now a group of Christians in this Kabyle village. They were sincere but frightened.

'They would burn the house down over our heads if ever we came right out for the Lord,' said his brother.

Meanwhile Abd alMasih had intervened with the French authorities and after many months the pension papers were renewed. Ali paid back the meagre five pounds that the missionary had lent him insisting that he would not accept this as a gift from a servant of God. It was rather he who should give. He was no 'rice Christian'. The hearts of Abd alMasih and Lalla Jouhra were warmed. This is what they had worked and prayed for. An indigenous church. Praise the Lord!

The strain of the past months had told severely on Ali. He realized to the full the cost of discipleship. 'If any man follow me, let him take up his cross.' The persistent opposition from his own people was hard for the sick man. The insults from his neighbours, the spitting and the cursing, the refusal to help with the roof when it leaked, were all as gall to this peace-loving man. He did rejoice that God had answered prayer and that he had his pension restored, his debts paid. He himself felt too weak to undertake the ten-mile journey over the mountains to withdraw his quarterly pension from the Post Office. This was where Abd alMasih felt sure that he could help. He would obtain a power of attorney and bring the money, but the Muslim population was determined to oppose to the end.

'A foreigner has no right to come into this Post Office,' the local postal authorities told him. They were Muslims and had to be heavily bribed before they would cash a money order. They knew that Abd alMasih would not do that! At any price the pension papers must be kept in their hands. In this way they could break the Kabyle Christian.

Then the bitter blow fell. Ali had entrusted the pension papers to his nephew and had instructed him to withdraw the money from the local Post Office. The nephew did not return. Days passed. Then he sent a message. He was so sorry, but on the way back from the Post Office the mule had wandered into the forest, and somehow the pension papers were lost, as well as the three months' allocation. Money, papers, everything were lost, and again Ali was a pauper. As he lay day after day in that bleak Kabyle hut and reflected on his lot, he lost his joy. He was at the mercy of these cruel relentless Muslims. Some of his family turned against him as no money was forthcoming. Drugs were placed in his food and his mind was affected. Deep depression set in. Unable to work, surrounded by enemies, stricken with T.B., yet still loving the Lord, he sank into the depths of despair. Abd alMasih tried to persuade him to come to town where he could obtain care and treatment, but no, he preferred to die in his own home.

There was only one thing that Abd alMasih could do. He could still visit him in his village, to read, comfort and pray with him. But when the servant of God arrived he found the door bolted and barred in the daytime, an unheard of thing in a Kabyle house. 'Ali, open the door', he called. He called again but there was no answer. A neighbour shouted, 'Ali, it is your friend, the Christian. He has come to see you.' The soul-chilling reply came back from the sick man. 'Tell him to go away. I have not a friend in the world.' Never will Abd alMasih forget the pathos of those words, the pang of sorrow that gripped his heart as, struggling to stifle the sobs and keep back the tears, he turned away. His only comfort was that in every pang that rends the heart the Man of Sorrows has a part.

Ali died a few days later, and was buried in a Muslim grave, although he had steadfastly refused to witness to Mohammed and had died a Christian. Even his enemies were compelled to admit that! His poor body lies in the Muslim cemetery just outside his village, one of the many who at the coming of the Lord will rise from Muslim cemeteries to meet the Lord in the air. He shall see of the travail of His soul and shall be satisfied. Surely that one soul was worth all the effort, the travail, the sorrow and pain, yet pain mingled with joy to see the manifest workings of the Holy Spirit!

> 'Come tell Me all that ye have said and done,
> Your victories and failures, hopes and fears;
> I know how hardly souls are wooed and won;
> My choicest wreaths are always wet with tears.'

North Africa has been called, 'The land of the vanished church', for there were formerly hundreds of Christian church buildings scattered along the northern coast of that great continent. Extensive ruins are to be found everywhere and large baptistries indicate that, in the early North African churches, baptism was by immersion. It is a most interesting coincidence that in each centre where Abd alMasih and his wife were used of God to lead Muslims to Christ, there had formerly been Christian Churches. Were these conversions the result of the prayers of Christians many centuries before? If this is so, how wonderful is the power of prayer! How far-reaching the answer!

In the early days of the Church the believers were scattered by persecution and the gospel was spread. In many places today, both in Algeria and in France, are to be found those who first heard the Word and believed when they were in Lesser Kabylia. They carry with them the living Word of God enabling them to be lights in the darkness. The Lord Jesus said, 'My sheep hear My voice, I know them . . . No man can pluck them out of My hand.' Thus the Lord assures us that He can and will keep His own sheep. They are isolated and often cut off from all Christian fellowship, yet there is abundant evidence that these isolated believers still love their Lord and ours. The struggle continues but the outcome is sure, for there is nothing too hard for God.

Chapter Thirteen

A Strategic Centre

It became increasingly evident that, whilst the major part of the population was being evangelised through the clinics and visits to villages, some means must be found to contact others who were enquiring about the things of God. Lafayette and Hammam were surrounded by Arab villages, but the first Kabyle villages were twenty miles away. The people came to Lafayette occasionally, but not regularly. Thus a centre in Kabylia was most desirable. It was obvious that the strategic centre was the big Friday market at Beni Ourtilane. This was held every week and would be attended by five thousand to ten thousand men according to the time of year. The difficulty was to get a piece of ground on which to erect a small building. To rent a room would have been to court disaster, for as soon as numbers of people began to attend, the owner would have given notice to quit.

In Kabylia the Old Testament law of redemption still holds good. Every effort is made to retain property or ground in the family. If a stranger purchases, any member of the family can step in and reclaim the land, paying back the purchase price. For this reason for many long years no missionary had been able to purchase ground in the mountains, but there is nothing too hard for God. Abd alMasih finally succeeded in finding a man who had no near kinsmen. From this man he purchased a large piece of ground on the outskirts of the market, near a fountain, and which bordered on two roads. There were thirty villages in the tribe, and numberless others in the tribes surrounding it.

As soon as it was possible to do so after the war, stone was quarried and the building started. A Hall seating forty-five people, a small room with two bunk beds and a garage were erected. Then the Hall was furnished.

At first the market place was surrounded by about forty buildings, with coffee houses, a baker's premises and administrative offices, but later there were also a large police station, schools and a dispensary.

An Eastern market is always an attraction. In the fruit and vegetable section huge piles of oranges, cabbages, water melons, potatoes, tomatoes and peppers tempt the prospective buyer. In the summer there are mountains of grapes, peaches and pomegranates, melons and prickly pears. The purchaser is allowed to turn over the fruit and pick out the best, rejecting any that is blemished or under standard. In another section each man has small leather sacks made from goats skins and containing lentils, beans or chick peas. There are mounds of wheat and barley. When measuring, the bushel is filled, and the corn piled up to form a cone. If the buyer can add another grain, he is at liberty to do so. Figs are lightly pressed into the measure. Oil is poured in until it runs over. The whole market area is filled with a motley throng of men. Not a woman or girl can be seen. Just outside the market some very old women sit with a few eggs for sale. The Arab doctor spreads his wares on a lion's skin. He has anything from bitter aloes to antimony to beautify the eyes. (Eye shadow was used in Algeria long before it came into fashion in England!) The dentist is there vaunting his ability to extract any tooth with his finger and thumb, without pain and without blood. A pile of teeth nearly a foot high testifies to his success. Droves of sheep, herds of bullocks and some goats crowd together in the animal section.

Each Friday morning Abd alMasih would travel up to Beni Ourtilane by car, leaving home soon after 5 a.m. On arrival he would sweep out the Hall, prepare his food, light a fire in winter, and wait for the boys. They would crowd in on their way to market, and he would have a class. This class would be taken in two or three successive sections, until sixty or seventy boys had been in. Then men would start calling in for advice, or a chat on spiritual things. At 10 or 10.30 a.m. he would go up to the market, walking round and chatting with friends, purchasing fruit and vegetables. Back again at the Hall, any who were interested would drop in for the reading of God's Word. Lakhdar, Yousef, Tehar, Ali and others trusted the Saviour in that little Hall.

In the afternoon Abd alMasih would shoulder his bag and walk to the surrounding villages, returning to his room for the night. Then early on Saturday morning the sick folk would start arriving. He would work on until midday or after, preaching, caring for the sick, performing minor operations as has already been described for Hammam. Whenever possible Lalla Jouhra would accompany him. She would visit the women and he the men, and then they would pass the night at Beni Ourtilane, sleeping in the bunk beds placed one over the other. Thus there was an ever-increasing outreach, and in all honesty it can be said that from fifty to sixty per cent of the population of the whole area heard the message of salvation.

Beni Ourtilane eventually served as the base for a further extension of the work. A rough motor road led past the Hall and on through the tribe to a group of five villages.

Abd alMasih often visited this group, and some of the men asked him if it would not be possible for him to live amongst them so that they could profit from a more continuous ministry. He therefore decided that, during the month of May, he would make a special effort of fifteen days' duration. The men arranged for him to have the use of a disused coffee house, rent free. He set up his camp bed in half of the building and put down some rush mats in the other section. The mornings were devoted to the care of the sick, the afternoons were spent in sitting with the men in the mosques; and when the boys came out of school a class was held for them. Then, after supper, the men of the five villages gathered to listen to a message.

It was a new experience, living alone among the people for a fortnight. Darkness fell. The sheikh had called to prayer. The room of the coffee house was ready. Abd alMasih had very carefully prepared the message that night, on the Deity of Christ. It is the bedrock truth of the gospel, but a most difficult subject to deal with. Not only must he speak the whole truth, but he must communicate to these men the fact that Jesus Christ is God. 'What think ye of Christ?' was the challenge. He proceeded to speak of His pre-existence, His virgin birth, His spotlessly pure life, His mighty power, His superlative titles, His atoning death, His glorious resurrection, His wonderful ascension, His present session at the right hand of God, and His glorious return. How would such a subject be received by this Muslim audience? They were living in the security of their environment, anticipating in their hearts a speedy victory in the war for Independence which they all knew would soon begin. Then Islam would reign supreme throughout their land. The servant of God had good cause to fear the outcome of such a talk at such a time. He was in their hands, sleeping in their village, in a loaned coffee house, with no locks to the doors. He was therefore conscious of his own utter weakness, yet with the conviction that God had committed to him this message, that he spoke that evening. The meeting closed and the men left.

Several men were lurking in the darkness. He could just discern their forms. They came back. So this was it. 'Lord help me to be faithful,' was his prayer. The first man approached. 'Sheikh, that was really wonderful. It is just what we all want to know.'

Another man came up. 'Tell us more like that. Thank you for that wonderful message.'

Yet another came. 'May God bless you. Our teachers never tell us anything like that. It did my heart good.'

Then came an offer not to be despised, 'I will place the large olive press and the adjoining room at your disposal. You can have them rent free as often as you like to come. Try and come to us every week.'

The heart of Abd alMasih leaped for joy. Is there anything too hard for God? These were the men who had so violently opposed the work when it started. Now they were providing means for a weekly meeting. So on Saturday afternoons he travelled down to that group of villages. The weekly programme was an afternoon clinic with messages, a men's meeting in the evening, and then a long journey in the dark along the narrow dangerous road skirted by steep precipices that led to Lafayette and home.

The Shepherd leads His servants to the lost sheep by a pathway that He Himself has trodden. 'Where I am there also shall My servant be,' indicates close fellowship with Him. He was on His way to the Cross. 'What shall I say? Father, save me from this hour? No, for this purpose I have come to this hour.' Souls can be sought and found only by the pathway of suffering, endurance and sacrifice. The servant must follow in the footsteps of his Lord. Thus the missionary is conscious of a growing appreciation of his relationship to the Lord Jesus. He is Lord of all, and the missionary is His willing bondslave, constantly looking to Him for guidance in his ministry and messages, and seeking increasingly to acknowledge His supremacy. He is also increasingly conscious that, in fellowship with His Lord, he is ostracised, unwanted and despised. A close intimacy develops between the Lord and His servant. The long years of arduous service, the hope deferred that makes the heart sick, may make him say in fellowship with the Lord, 'I have laboured in vain, I have spent my strength for nought and in vain.' He shares the heartbreak of Him who wept over Jerusalem.

Aith Moussa is a large village situated in the mountains of Kabylia. Every two months Abd alMasih visited this group of villages, leaving the hall at Beni Ourtilane after the market, spending the night in a Kabyle house, and returning early the following morning. Going into the first village he heard a voice, 'O sheikh. Come over here. We badly need you.'

The oxen had been fighting and the eye of one had been gored out. He was asked to treat the suppurating wound. Then he was taken to a girl in the throes of fever, an old lady with a violent cough, and finally a woman with bad eyes. Abd alMasih noted the names in his book, told the man to bring some bottles to the dispensary next day, and went on to the coffee house. It was full of men playing dominoes and cards. They were sitting on mats round low tables, smoking and talking loudly. The atmosphere was that of an English public house. Removing his shoes and leaving them with those of the men outside the door, he found his way across the mats to a position where he could see all the men, and seated himself.

'What will you have, sheikh, coffee or tea?'

'Coffee, please.'

'How would you like it? Sweet, sweet bitter, strong, or just right?'

'Give me a *gedged* please.' A gedged is just right, not too sweet, not too bitter, but almost thick enough for the small spoon in it to stand up alone! Sipping his coffee he waited. The men at the next table had finished their games. Then another group finished. He was conscious that all the men were silent and watching him intently. Then one man sitting wrapped round in his long woollen burnous spoke up.

'Now, sheikh, we're waiting for you. Get out the Book and read to us again.' There was no need to tell him which book, he carried only one. Amid murmurs of approval they listened to the message. Half an hour passed. The message was direct, pointed and aimed at leading them to trust in the living Saviour who died for them. Having finished the message he prepared to leave.

'How much for the coffee?' he asked.

'That is paid for, sheikh. We Kabyles do not let our teachers pay for coffee. Don't be too long before you return.'

As he passed on to the next village he reflected that in civilised England, he would scarcely receive such a welcome in a public house, and yet every two months when he returned to that village the men put down their games, and asked him to speak to them. This was no isolated case, for in nearly half of the coffee houses he found the same attitude to his message. What a change from those early years! He reflected that in England dear brethren are asking the Lord to bring just one unsaved person into the hall (although that person seldom comes). Yet at the weeknight prayer meeting those same devout brethren will tell the Lord how hard it is to reach Muslims with the gospel! 'Lord, Thou knowest, they don't want to listen.' Satan's lie still persists, 'Muslims do not want the gospel.'

'He could there do no mighty work because of their unbelief,' the unbelief of believers! Reflecting thus he passed on to the last village.

The sun was sinking in a ball of fire beneath the horizon. The voice of the muezzin calling the faithful to prayer rang out. It was time for Abd alMasih to finish his message. He distributed a few books to those who could read, and waited until prayers were finished. He was quite sure that in a few moments someone would offer him shelter for the night and an evening meal. Prayers over, the men left the mosque, walked past him without a word and went to their homes. A fresh cold wind blew down from the high mountain overshadowing the village. The shepherd boys came in with their sheep and goats, whistling, prodding, urging them on. A man with a couple of bullocks moved by, carrying on his shoulder the heavy wooden plough. He passed through the massive wooden doors of the courtyard in front of which Abd alMasih was sitting and shortly afterwards closed them with a thud. The heavy wooden bolts were slipped into place. Then all was silent. Darkness fell. One by one he heard the head of each house shut the door, securing it with the massive bars. No one would go out until morning. Then the head of each house would reopen the door and it would stay open all day. Inside the houses the mats had been laid out, and the families would soon be spreading their beds and retiring for the night. The scene was so familiar to him. He had so often shared their fire, partaken of their meal and enjoyed their fellowship. But tonight he was shut out. He waited on. The cry of the sheikh again rang out through the pitch black night. It was *Laacha*, the last prayer of the day, one hour after sunset. From some homes came the low murmur of voices as the family drew closer to the warmth of the fire and discussed the events of the day. It was cold in these mountains when the sun set. Abd alMasih sat and shivered in that cold mountain air.

There was no doubt in his mind now. This was a studied insult. The laws of Kabyle hospitality had been ignored, the guest left outside in the cold. Abd alMasih realised that he must find his way back over those bleak cold mountains. Through the sleeping village he walked. Even the dogs were silent. It was pitch black. He walked on through the cemetery, past the tombs. He climbed up the rough pathway strewn with stones and boulders. Now and again he stumbled and nearly fell. What was that? He stiffened. It was only the screech of an owl as it flew near to his head, from close by a jackal howled, and it was answered by several others just below the road. He was hungry, utterly weary and chilled to the bone by the icy wind. Up and up he climbed until he reached the place where the path narrowed to a couple of feet. Below was a sheer drop of five hundred feet. His nailed boots slipped on the polished surface of the rock. He pulled himself together. It would not do to get the jitters now. Again the ominous hoot of a night bird pierced the air. No Kabyle man would take such a journey at night over those mountains alone. Yet . . . he was not alone! 'I will never leave you nor forsake you.' The verse rang continuously in his mind. A sweet assurance from his ever-present Lord. Yet he still felt terribly alone. He meditated on that time in the life of the Lord Jesus when 'they went every man to his own house, but Jesus went to the Mount of Olives'. Utterly spent he sat on a rock and looked down to the villages far below. Here and there a light flickered. The sounds of village life still came up, a few men were still moving round down there. But he was cast out, rejected, hated, because he was associated with a rejected Lord. He prayed for those men . . . and then unashamedly wept.

He finally reached his room in the early hours of the

morning, and threw himself on the bed, utterly weary and sad at heart, discouraged because of the hardness of the way. Why does God in His infinite wisdom permit such heartbreaks? Surely to bring His servants into closer fellowship with Himself, to allow them to enter more fully into the fellowship of His sufferings.

There is however a sequel to this story. The following morning Abd alMasih was awakened from sleep and called from his bed quite early. *'Sebah alkheyr, ya sheikh'* (Good morning, sheikh). 'Hurry up and open the door. I have brought the bottles. Give me my medicine at once and let me get back to work.' It was one of the men from the village to which he had gone the previous day.

The Hall filled up and Abd alMasih commenced his message. The Kabyle mind is always alert and quick to grasp the meaning of a parable, and Abd alMasih decided to use this painful incident as an apt illustration. He began,

'This morning I have a story to tell you all. Yesterday I met a man in a village who greatly values my medicines. He is here this morning. Last night I sat outside his door. He saw me and knew that I needed shelter and warmth, but he left me sitting in the street, outside his house, at his door. He really wanted my medicines. He ardently desired what I had to give him, but he did not want me. This morning he has come to the door of my house, and he expects me to receive him and give him anything that he asks for.

'Now may I read to you all from the Word of God? The Lord Jesus says, "Behold, I stand at the door and knock; if any one hears My voice, and opens the door, I will come in to him and eat with him, and he with Me." Today the Lord Jesus stands at your heart's door. You know that He wants to come in. You want His gifts. You like to listen to His

Word, but you leave Him outside. You reject Him. Listen
again. The same Lord Jesus says, "When once the house-
holder has risen up and shut the door, you will begin to
knock at the door saying, Lord, Lord, open to us." He will
answer you, "I do not know where you come from," then
you will begin to say, "We ate and drank in Your presence
and You taught in our streets," but He will say, "I tell you, I
do not know where you come from, depart from Me, all
you workers of iniquity" (Luke 13:25–27 RSV). Those are
His words to you now. Tomorrow you will be standing at
His door. What will He say to you then, if today you have
refused to admit Him into your hearts? Now go back to
your village, and take this message with you and tell it to
all.'

The following market day several leading men of that
village called to express their regret at the incident, asking
Abd alMasih to return and to spend the night in their
house. He did so the following week, for love is not resent-
ful, love bears all things, believes all things, hopes all
things, endures all things. But it had hurt to be left out in
the cold, and the more so because he loved them.

'O Abd alMasih, witness to Mohammed!' (see page 40)

In the market

Beni Ourtilane market

Chapter Fourteen

The Valley of the Shadow

The Berber populations of Algeria are very intelligent and able to compete with Europeans in every walk of life yet, owing to the presence of over one million European settlers, Algeria was not granted independence until after seven long years of sanguinary strife. The Lord's servant will always refrain from meddling in politics, and remain strictly neutral during a civil war, but it is quite impossible to continue to work for God at such a time without feeling the repercussions. Time and again the missionaries' hearts were grieved to see the brutalities committed by both sides. Yet in the goodness of God, His work continued and His faithfulness and power were constantly evident.

The struggle for independence commenced on November 1st 1954, when Europeans travelling in the Aures mountains were ambushed and, in Kabylia, stacks of cork were fired and police posts attacked. For some months the war was limited. Cars were held up and machine-gunned; individuals were threatened that they would be killed if they did not obey orders. Many were mutilated by the removal of ears or noses, or were otherwise maimed. At the outset the whole movement was political, but it was fomented by the religious leaders who proclaimed it to be a 'holy war'. During 1955 bands of insurgents armed with guns, knives and sub-machine guns roamed the whole country, but were to be found chiefly in the mountainous regions of Kabylia and the Aures. The work at Lafayette and the three outstations continued during this period, and Abd alMasih was able to make a special effort, reaching two hundred and fifty villages during the course of the year.

Abd alMasih had been warned. The village was situated in a lonely part of the country amidst the Aleppo pines, surrounded by steep precipitous slopes of scree and shale. 'It would be wiser not to go there,' he was told. 'Last year they killed twelve men, simply murdered them in cold blood. They are paid assassins. For as little as five pounds they will undertake to kill a man by poisoning or by shooting him, but they usually charge fifty. They are dangerous, and not to be trusted, so mind your step.' Abd alMasih listened. Should he go on in spite of the warning? Yet they were men for whom Christ died. But how could he approach them? With some trepidation he entered the village and chatted with the men. Then he opened his Bible and read from Galatians. 'The fruit of the Spirit is love, joy, peace, longsuffering, gentleness, goodness, faith, meekness, temperance, against such there is no law. Now the works of the flesh are adultery . . . hatred, variance . . . envyings, murders . . .' Here he paused.

'Is it possible that there are murderers in this village?' he asked.

'There are forty or more. Nearly every man in this village has taken life,' was the solemn reply. They listened quietly to the Word of God, but the silence was almost ominous. He left their village and went back to his car which he had left by the roadside.

Below the road was another very large village. Should he go down to the men there? Ten years earlier he had visited it with a fellow-worker, and they had been chased from the village, sent off with vile words. Now he was alone. He turned aside into the bush to pray. Below he could see the men as they went in and out of the mosque, looking as small as ants. Yet his heart almost failed him for fear. How could he go alone? Taking out his pocket New Testament one sentence leapt at him, 'I can do all things through Christ Who strengthens me.' Still anxious and fearful, but assured by the promise, he went down to face the bitter opposition. It did not come. Instead, eighty men gathered and listened intently to the message. There were also unseen listeners of whom he knew nothing. (Nearly a year later, in a village more than fifty miles away, a woman told Lalla Jouhra she had listened that day and had believed.

'Do you know that man who spoke in our village?' she asked Lalla Jouhra. 'You say just the same things as he did.'

'He is my husband,' was the reply.

'Well, our men cannot forget the message that your husband gave them that day. For weeks they talked it over in their homes.'

How good is the God we serve! How very gracious of Him to use His fearful, hesitating servants!)

The sun was setting as Abd alMasih wended his way back to the tent which had been pitched by the road side. He was met by his Kabyle man.

'*Laselama, ya sheikh*' (Return in peace, teacher). 'There is no need for me to light the primus tonight. They have sent across couscous and meat from the village' (the assassins' village).

'Praise God for that,' said Abd alMasih. 'Get out two plates and we will eat together.'

He replied 'No, sheikh, it is all for you. I have eaten my portion.' Abd alMasih insisted that they should eat together as they had done each day but the Kabyle was adamant. 'Then you can pitch the stuff into the ravine.' There was no doubt about it. The food was poisoned.

The next day he visited several villages, and the Kabyle man returned across the mountains to his home. Abd alMasih was to spend the last night alone, only a few miles away from the assassins' village. He chose the spot where he was to camp for the night. It was over four thousand feet above sea level, delightfully situated in the middle of a lovely fragrant forest of pines. The slopes of the mountain fell away steeply to the deep ravines, where wild boar roamed. It was one of the most rugged and wild parts of the country. There was just one house nearby, and the Post Office. He could always get water there, and he would be near a Government employee. The situation throughout the country was acute and feelings were running high. Many had lost their lives during the first months of this sad war. But, 'the night comes when no man can work'. He must go on. He left the car on the road, and again scrambled down the steep stony pathway to the mosque where the men had gathered.

The sun was almost on the horizon as he left the hamlet and found his way back to the car. A fierce Arab dog persisted in following him. This shaggy dog came so near that he felt most uneasy. So often he had been attacked by these half-wild animals which leap at the throat. They were never friendly to a stranger. Standing with his back to a wall he would swing his bag until someone came to call the dogs off, but here in the mountain there was no one to help. He deliberately stoned the dog, time and again, but the dog persisted in following. Climbing up the steep mountain path, almost panting for breath, he finally reached the car. The dog still followed. He drove along to the forester's house but not a soul could be seen. Then he called in at the Post Office, but to his dismay, there was no one there either. He learned later that it was far too dangerous for the Post Office official to spend the night in that isolated spot at such a time. The man and his family slept in the village on the lower slopes.

There was an uncanny feeling of stillness as Abd alMasih unlocked the car, got out the tent and pitched it, set up his camp bed and lit the primus. The dog was still there, prowling round at a distance, but getting closer. It looked like a huge grey wolf in the twilight. One more attempt to drive it off with stones, and it slunk away. Abd alMasih cooked a little macaroni for supper and then took one last look around before he turned in for the night. That wretched dog was still there, looking so fierce and threatening that he made yet another effort to drive it away, pelting it with a volley of stones. The sun had set, darkness fell. Not a single person was about. The road was deserted. It was uncanny.

Abd alMasih was dead tired. He stretched himself out on his camp bed and fell sound asleep. At midnight he was awakened by a strange noise. He sat up in his bed and flashed on his pocket lamp; to his dismay he saw the savage dog had crawled into the tent and was fast asleep beside the bed! What was that? A twig cracked, someone was about. The dog growled. He again switched on his pocket lamp and had a good look round. To his utter astonishment the bread and macaroni which he had left from supper were on the plate under his bed untouched! He had been so tired that he had dropped off to sleep, leaving the food under his bed. He rubbed his eyes, it seemed incredible! The food was still there, untouched by the savage, half-famished dog. At daybreak he was up and, calling the dog outside, gave it the food which it quickly ate. A quick wash, followed by a cup of coffee and he struck the tent, storing it in the car. Before he started the engine he turned and saw his faithful friend, the dog which he had so cruelly stoned, trotting away down the mountain path, wagging its tail with evident pleasure, its task complete. Why did the dog follow so persistently the one who treated it so badly? Who sent it? You may have your own theories, but Abd alMasih is sure that the God who cared for Daniel, cared for him that night. Danger was near, the Lord knew and cared for his servant. Abd alMasih had proved Him for so long and in so many situations that he knew the promise, 'Lo, I am with you alway,' is no idle word. Just why He should send a dog on that occasion, he may never know, but he knows Him enough to trust His wisdom, love and power.

This was the last tour that he made to distant villages. The weekly visits to Beni Ourtilane continued, and each Friday afternoon was spent in the surrounding villages. A good number of men had gathered at Houria and Abd alMasih remained until sunset before leaving for home. An hour's walk lay between him and the little room near the market, a stiff climb up the hill. Darkness quickly fell, and it was impossible to see more than a few feet ahead. Suddenly he heard the sound of muffled footsteps, and before he realised what was happening, he was surrounded by a band of sturdy youths. A light shone on his face for an instant, and someone exclaimed, 'Why, it is sheikh.'

'Sheikh, are you not afraid to be out alone at night with all that is happening around?' they said.

'I am not alone,' was the reply. In a moment they were on the alert and peered into the darkness. Suddenly they realised just what his words implied. He had an unseen Companion.

'No, sheikh, of course you are not alone. *Ror ek alhaq* (You are right). Go in peace, and may God make your way easy!' So back he went to his lonely outpost, and to bed.

The lonely night journey back from the group of five villages each Saturday was a tremendous challenge. Should he continue to travel back regularly every Saturday night? Surely to do so would be to court disaster. But 'Behold I have set before thee an open door.' 'The night cometh.' At this time road blocks were frequent. Large stones or trees would be placed across the road, and this would compel the driver of a car or bus to stop his vehicle. The next morning the blackened, burned-out hulk of the car, and the mutilated bodies of the occupants, told their own sad tale. Outside the towns no one moved after dark. The nationals openly boasted, 'The country is ours after sunset. We control everything.'

It was nine o'clock at night. The men's meeting was over and Abd alMasih was driving his car, following the winding road, back to his home at Lafayette. At a turning, the car lights lit up the large stones that had been placed right across the road, completely blocking it. The stones were much too large to allow the car to pass. There was an eerie stillness. Quickly he breathed a prayer, 'Lord, I am Yours. The work is Yours. Get me through somehow.' Then he saw that by driving the car into the ditch he could just get through. 'Praise the Lord.' Another ten miles and he was nearly home. 'Halt, hands up.' A bright light shone in his eyes and dazzled him, the muzzle of a tommy-gun was pointed at his chest. '*Qui est-ce?*' (Who is it?). It was the local gendarmes keeping a lookout on the road just below their headquarters.

'It is very unsafe to travel at night, *Monsieur le Pasteur*. Better wait until this little trouble is over. It will go on only for a week or so. You know that in Kabylia, after dark, you are in their hands.' So they thought, but he knew that he was in stronger, wiser, better hands.

So the work went on. By the end of the year over a

hundred thousand security forces were in Algeria, but in spite of this the atrocities multiplied. Both sides were involved. Rival bands roamed the land. Plunder, rape, arson and murder were the order of the day. Personal grievances of long standing, tribal feuds, religious animosity and false accusations, were all made the excuse for widespread slaughter. But the work of God continued.

Abd alMasih will never forget his last visit to the little Hall in the mountains. Friday morning had been spent with visitors from the market, and the afternoon in the villages. Saturday was a public holiday and he realised that few would come to the dispensary. He left the shelter of his little home at 4 a.m., just as dawn was breaking over the lovely mountains, the mountains where death lurked in every ravine and from every high crest. Driving along the road for eight miles through blackened forest, which had been burned down so that it would not provide shelter for an ambush, he parked the car on the side of the road, in a deserted spot, miles from any village, and committed it to the care of God, the One Who had never failed him. Shouldering his bag of tracts and New Testaments, he started to tramp over the rough road. It was completely deserted. An hour's walk brought him to the first village. An old man asked, 'What happened last night? The powder spoke.' Abd alMasih assured him that he knew nothing. It transpired later that a band of men had held up the bus travelling down from the market. They had gone on to set fire to the bulldozer that was making a new road, had taken prisoner the four watchmen and had passed the night in the very group of villages in which he now found himself. Of this Abd alMasih knew nothing.

The men were in good humour. Thirty gathered in each of the two first villages. Not a word was said of any trouble and they listened well to the message, thanking him warmly for still going to them at such a time. He crossed the little valley to the other side and, as he talked to the men in this village, he heard someone calling from a distance. Not until then did he see that the whole mountain was alive with troops. Then he was informed of all that had happened the preceding night. The troops and the burned-out bulldozer were between him and the car. Other vehicles had been destroyed, but the little car was intact, watched over by invisible eyes, in safe keeping indeed.

Abd alMasih ate his sandwiches and moved on to the last village. Exactly sixteen men gathered and sat on the stones of the public meeting place in the open air. Every detail of the scene stands out clearly in his mind until this day. The knoll rising steeply behind him, with the burned-out bulldozer on top. Hundreds of troops surrounding it, machine guns at the ready. It was obvious that after he had given the message he must face the music. What a solemn setting for a gospel meeting! He reminded his hearers that the wages of sin is death, of their need of forgiveness and of the One who had brought forgiveness and salvation.

Meanwhile the troops were hurling great boulders down the mountain side into the ravine which bordered the village. Suddenly the crack of a machine gun broke through the stillness. Were they firing at the little group? No it was only meant to scare them. The bullets were directed into the ravine yards to their right. The immediate reaction in such circumstances is to take cover, but one of the villagers turned to his friends and said, 'Stay where you are, all of you. They are watching us.' Then, turning to Abd alMasih he said, 'Sheikh, carry on. Finish your message.'

That was the hardest thing he had ever had to do, but the message was given, the last he was ever to give in that village. He shook hands with them all and said 'Goodbye'. Then he had to go and face the authorities. He found the military gathered round the wreck of the bulldozer. The local gendarmes saw him and exclaimed, 'It is Monsieur le Pasteur! We thought it was a rebel leader.' Abd alMasih expressed his sincere regret at such wanton destruction. It was obvious that the military were distinctly annoyed with him. Appearances were all against him. It seemed that he was hand-in-glove with the opposing forces.

The following week the whole area surrounding Beni Ourtilane and those villages was evacuated by the French Army, and a control post was established just below Lafayette. Sadly, Abd alMasih realised that the people of those five hundred villages which he had visited so regularly for so many years had heard the Good News for the last time. The night had come, the night when no man can work.

From their house Abd alMasih and Lalla Jouhra watched the long convoy as it wound its way into Lafayette. It was composed of army lorries, laden with equipment and furniture from European homes, and accompanied by tanks and armoured cars. They realised that the French army had evacuated Lesser Kabylia. The road to Beni Ourtilane was cut in over forty places by the Nationalist army, the bridges were blown up and every European building in the area was destroyed. Every school, post office, forester's house and farm was burned to the ground. Systematic bombing of the villages was carried out by the other side. The whole area, where for over thirty years Abd alMasih had gone about preaching and caring for the sick, was now a battlefield. The outstations in the mountains were in the hands of the nationalists. They could no longer be visited.

Some of the villages were pro-French and others had

Nationalist sympathies. Whole villages were devastated and, in some places, the whole population perished. A survivor from one village said, 'They suddenly came on us and demanded food and shelter. They took the very best of everything. All our young men were taken as conscripts for the army. Our animals were driven away. We were compelled to empty our store cupboards of figs, corn and oil.'

The bands were tracked down by aircraft, attacked with rockets, bombs and machine guns. Many villages were reduced to heaps of smoking ruins.

After five months the French army fought its way back to Beni Ourtilane. They found the Hall intact. God had preserved it through the fighting and bombing. The Muslims had respected it as a house of God. They had heard the Word of God there. There they had prayed and had seen something of the love of Christ in action. It stood alone among the ruins, a silent testimony to the power of love. A Christian man was present when the army destroyed it. It was deliberately smashed to pieces and everything it contained was destroyed.

For many months permission to visit it was refused, but eventually Abd alMasih was allowed to travel up to Beni Ourtilane with a French army convoy. What a sad sight met his eyes! All doors and window frames had been taken away and burned. The dividing walls between the Hall and the rest room were broken down. The floor was a mass of Scripture portions, tiles, saucepans, broken crockery, twisted bedsteads and broken chairs, bottles of medicine, ointments and Bibles. So much hard work had been put into the building of that outstation. It had been the missionaries' home in the mountains for years, a lighthouse from which radiated the rays of Divine truth. Now the light was extinguished, the house and Hall were in ruins. Was it another knock-out blow? Paul says, 'We may be knocked down but we are never knocked out. We are always facing death, but this means that you know more and more of life.' He got up and fought on.

The door to Kabylia was closed. The Bible Society knew that Abd alMasih had translated the four Gospels into the dialect of Lesser Kabylia and that this translation had been very well received. They had therefore asked him, just before hostilities started, to be responsible for the revision of the Kabyle New Testament. There were many unfortunate mistakes in the first translation, and these had to be corrected and the whole New Testament thoroughly revised. God had set him free from his very busy life as an evangelist in order that he might devote his time to the even more important work of translation for which He had been equipping him for the past thirty years. A committee was formed of nationals and missionaries. Now he was able to push ahead with this work. But committee meetings meant that he must travel on roads made dangerous by the opposing sides in the civil war. Once more he was cast on a faithful God for protection. Many missionaries deemed it foolhardy to travel, but for Abd alMasih there was no choice for, if the consultants over the large area were to be contacted, and they were unable or unwilling to travel, then he must go to them. But how? Should a servant of God travel with the protection of a military escort? Or should he continue those long perilous journeys trusting in the living God? Surely the attitude of Ezra should be his! 'I was ashamed to require of the king a band of soldiers and horsemen to help us against the enemy in the way, because we had spoken ... saying, "The hand of our God is upon all them for good that seek him." ' The Kabyles and Arabs were fully aware of his attitude, and respected him for it. Down through the years a Muslim who became a Christian had always had to face the possibility of death. The Christian missionary was never an apostate, and was therefore immune from danger and death. Now the glorious opportunity had come to adopt an attitude of strict neutrality, of absolute dependence on God, and to give practical proof that the God he served was able to deliver . . . 'He will deliver, but if not . . .' The possibility had to be faced. If He did not deliver, he would go to be with the Lord. 'I will fear no evil, for You are with me.'

The journey to Les Ouadhias necessitated a special pass. Two roads leading to the area were so dangerous that they were forbidden to all but military vehicles. One road remained. The evidences of war were on every hand. There were block houses in every village from which guns peered through, lookout towers, military patrols, the rattle of machine guns, the boom of heavy artillery, the roar of low-flying aircraft and helicopters. After six hours' travelling over dangerous and deserted roads, Abd alMasih reached the mission station in the heart of Kabylia where two single missionary sisters were bravely carrying on. The house was outside the protected perimeter of the village. Every window and door was sand-bagged to give some protection from flying bullets. A new house was under construction, but there were no locks to the doors. Here he was to spend the nights; work during the day was in the new building.

'You cannot lock yourself in at night,' said the lady missionary as she showed him his room. 'The Kabyle men who are decorating the house will be sleeping below in another room. Fighting goes on all round right through the night.' 'What are those small holes in the walls?' enquired Abd alMasih.

'Oh, just bullet holes. Last night one came in here and went out there, and the other lodged in that pillar.'

The lady left and Abd alMasih bent down to line up the

two holes where the bullet had come in and gone out. It would have passed immediately over his pillow, two inches higher than his head. He turned the bed round the other way!

It was 10 p.m. The boom of heavy artillery shelling a distant village, the rattle of machine guns close at hand and the plop plop of shotguns from the nationalists were heard. Quite suddenly a pack of jackals started to yelp and howl, their voices echoed through the uncanny stillness of the night. Jackals? So many, and so near? Abd alMasih crept from his bed to the shutters and peered into the darkness. He could just discern in the pale moonlight the dusky forms of the men preparing to attack the military post. So these were the jackals! Thus gradually he found the meaning of the cries of the night, the howling dog, the hoot of the owl and many more. The long night passed, and morning came.

During the day the work of revision went on. 'The Son of man . . .' Shall we change that word for man? Is Jesus the Son of a man? If so, of what man? Should it not rather be, '*Emmis m bounadem?*' linking Him thus with the human race? The blind consultant and the missionary worked on from early morning until sunset, almost without a break, and, as they worked, the battle raged.

The last committee meeting for the Kabyle New Testament was held at Azazga in the heart of Kabylia and in a war zone. No missionary or consultant would leave his home to travel by public or private transport. It was too risky. Buses were burned out, trains derailed every day. Nevertheless, the meeting must be held before the MS could be completed and sent off. Blind Jules was approached and said, 'I will travel if you come and fetch me, not otherwise.' So the long journey of fifty kilometres was made. Not a single soul could be seen. Even military patrols were absent, and the bridges were unguarded, yet the sense of danger, of evil, lurked everywhere. Then on to Azazga with another Kabyle consultant, and up to a Kabyle village to find yet another helper. The six members of the committee were complete. Two other missionaries would not leave their homes. Why should they endanger their lives? The last decisions were made, the MS adapted and despatched, and the proofs awaited.

A short furlough followed. Oh! the relief to be right away from the tensions of war, away from the searchlights that swept the whole village every night, the hideous howl of the wounded dog, the yapping of the jackals, the lone call of the owl (every sound significant), the rattle of machine guns as someone broke the curfew and paid the price, or the bursting of bombs, the sounds of torture, . . .

The furlough quickly passed and Africa called. Should they go back?

If you had been to Muslim lands
Where suffering men stretch out their hands
To plead, yet no one understands;
Would you go back, would you?

If you had trod through Afric's sand
Your hand within the Saviour's hand
And knew He'd called you to that land;
Would you go back, would you?

If you had seen the women bear
Their heavy loads with none to share,
Had heard them weep with none to care;
Would you go back, would you?

If you had seen the Christian die
And stand for Christ when none was nigh,
Had seen him smile and say 'Goodbye';
Would you go back, would you?

Yet still they wait, a listless throng,
Longing for one to right their wrong.
When shall despair be turned to song?
We're going back. Would you?

(Adapted. Author unknown.)

So, back again they went – and what a welcome they received! On the night of their arrival at Lafayette there was a terrible storm and a cloudburst. The small stream which flowed through Hammam became a raging torrent. It rose twenty feet high, sweeping over the bridge in the centre of the village. The bridge collapsed and was swept away, one whole section of the village being engulfed and many losing their lives. Abd alMasih arrived just in time to see the last wall of the little Hall collapse and slide into the river. Everything disappeared in the raging torrent.

God had allowed the work at Hammam to continue until this fourth year of the war for Independence. For two and a half years it was situated in 'no man's land,' and to visit it Abd alMasih had to go out beyond the last French outpost. Hammam itself was visited by rebel bands nearly every night. Numbers attending the clinics had been slightly less than in normal years, but the Word of God had been a comfort to many. Now the Hall, where for nearly thirty-four years the gospel had been preached, was destroyed, carried away by the hand of God. It seemed another knockout blow. There was no possibility of recommencing work either at Hammam or at Beni Ourtilane. The army authorities refused permission to rebuild. Within a few days of the flood, fighting broke out in Hammam, all the men were imprisoned, and it would have been quite impossible to continue the work.

Until this time Abd alMasih's life had been remarkably full. Often twenty or even twenty-five groups of people would come under his ministry each week. Now God had set him free for the work for which He had been preparing him through the years. He makes no mistakes. His timing is perfect. Again, at the request of the Bible Society, he undertook to supervise a committee for the adaptation of the Moroccan Bible for use throughout North Africa. This translation work entailed more long journeys by road, but with an even closer sense of the Lord's presence and keeping power. During the long absences of her husband Lalla Jouhra carried on the work at Lafayette alone. What stories she had to tell!

On one occasion one thousand men were suddenly billeted in the village. The officer insisted that some must be billeted in the missionaries' house or in the Hall. Lalla Jouhra was alone, Abd alMasih was in Algiers. Twenty soldiers were duly installed in the Hall. Throughout the night the sentry tramped up and down. In the Hall the men slept or smoked. How could Lalla Jouhra continue classes and meetings in such conditions? Each week two hundred children were coming to learn God's Word. The boys insisted that they were men, and should not be turned out of their *jema* (mosque). They assured Lalla Jouhra that they were not going to be intimidated by soldiers. So, with men of the French army in the next room, they sang all the French hymns that they knew, she gave the message in the same language, and some hearts at least were touched. One of the men was seen listening outside with tears in his eyes.

A few days later the whole male population of Lafayette was behind barbed-wire entanglements, surrounded by soldiers with fierce dogs and tommy guns. They were kept there for more than a week, hungry, dirty, chilled to the bone, cowed and embittered. They thought of their unprotected homes, of the uncouth soldiers going from house to house, sometimes emptying all the food on the floor: wheat, barley, figs and oil, then pouring paraffin on the heap of food and setting fire to it. The reason for this was that they were accused of feeding rebels during the night. These men thought of their women folk, who were now at the mercy of the military, with no one to protect them. Suddenly they stared. Along the street came a band of soldiers, herding before them a mass of frightened women, who were clutching at their veils and flimsy dresses in a vain attempt to cover themselves and shield their babies. They were accustomed to the absolute privacy of their homes, and now ... Squads of men went from quarter to quarter of the village driving out the women, who were so reluctant to leave.

A little girl came flying in to Lalla Jouhra, panting for breath, terrified at all that was happening. She poured out her heart, 'They are taking all the women, just leaving us girls behind alone. What can we do? Where can we go? Pray, pray, pray for us. We know Jesus will save us. He will protect us. Pray for us.' Then she dashed off like an arrow to help her younger sister. To whom could she turn in her hour of distress, but to one who could pray, to Lalla Jouhra who so often had prayed for them and with them in their homes?

God's protective care of His servants impressed many Muslims at this time. Many were thinking deeply, but fear: fear of reprisals, fear of the unknown future, fear of breaking with Islam, kept them back from faith in the Lord Jesus.

As the situation became worse the whole town was surrounded with barbed-wire entanglements to keep out the enemy. At night men of the national army would come and cut through the barbed-wire. They entered the nearest Kabyle house to the mission station. The occupant had been warned and fled for his life. Everything that he possessed was piled in a heap in the middle of the floor and fired. Then they opened fire on the French forces, firing across the back garden of the Mission. Under such conditions the work of God went on. Every week fifty veiled Muslim women came to the clinic. They were the mothers of the children who attended the classes. Boys and girls came to the classes, even when bombs were falling half a mile away. Past the sentries they came, their happy singing in strange contrast to the din of the great helicopters that roared overhead and the bursting bombs.

The most terrifying experience for Lalla Jouhra was when she was alone in the house for nearly a week. Just over fifty yards away was an isolated military post, manned by a French N.C.O. and a dozen Arab men. The men were not allowed to retain their arms at night. 'Sergeant, come and look. Listen! The enemy is approaching. Give us our rifles.' The sergeant came from the shelter of his room, was attacked from behind by the men and literally hacked to pieces. His shrieks and cries pierced the night. The Arab men left their post, defecting to the rebel army, taking their arms with them. No one came to the help of the dying man. How terrifying for Lalla Jouhra, alone in her home! Yet she was not alone, for He has said, 'I will never leave you nor forsake you.' And so she could boldly say, even at such a time, 'I will not fear. What can man do to me?' Here was a true partnership. Abd alMasih facing danger on the roads as he travelled for the translation work, and Lalla Jouhra willingly accepting the responsibility of the Lord's work during his absence, and facing similar danger at home.

The Bible Society again appealed to Abd alMasih, this time to complete the New Testament in Algerian Arabic. The situation had changed almost overnight. The European settlers had revolted. In the centre of Algiers they had thrown up barricades, had occupied the whole block of University buildings, and Frenchmen armed with modern weapons faced Frenchmen. Every available man was sent down to Algiers. The radio proclaimed a state of public emergency. This was the day on which the last series of committee meetings for the Algerian Arabic New Testament were to begin. Again Abd alMasih was in a quandary. Should he dare to make the journey? It was yet another challenge to faith. Would these translations ever be used? The doors were closing fast. '*Madame, votre mari est fou*' (Madame, your husband is mad), said the French people when they heard he had ventured on the roads. Folly in the eyes of the world, but when God sends, and calls and protects, there really is no danger.

Every road junction was closely guarded. Tanks lined the roads overlooking the railways. Troops were everywhere.

'Halt! Get out of your car. Hands up! Well over your head!', the sentry ordered.

A thorough search of the car followed.

'Where are you going?'

'To Algiers.'

'But Algiers is surrounded by troops. You will never get in. No one is allowed in.'

'I can but try.'

'Well, if you are fool enough to try, you can carry on. *Bon voyage*! but you will not reach Algiers today'.

'Lord, you must get me through. You have never, no never, let me down. Lord, it is Your work and not mine.'

Thus the servant committed all to his never-failing Lord. Twenty times on that journey he was held up, the car was searched, he was searched. Then came the crucial test – Menerville. He passed through the town and then saw the three successive control posts, army – gendarmes – army. There was no doubt about it. Here they really meant business. Slowing up as he reached the first control post,

Abd alMasih took his wallet and papers from his pocket. Could he believe his eyes? The sentry waved him on! He was two hundred miles from home and in a strange country. No one knew him. Surely the civil police would stop him. Incredible though it may seem, they too waved him on! The same thing at the third control! He was through the crucial spot and had not even been asked to show his papers! He neared the capital city and again the car was searched. They suspected the typewriter, but they found no weapons, no grenades, no bombs. He was through. Algiers was like a city of the dead. Glass littered the streets. No one moved. Buildings were in ruins. The committee meeting started only half an hour behind scheduled time!

The committee worked on for a week. Each day men were murdered on the road outside. One day the gutters ran with human blood. Fifteen schools went up in flames in a single day. Beautiful villas were blasted every hour. It was a city of death, of dying, despairing men and women. The servants of God worked at the translation of the Living Word, the Word which was to bring cheer and comfort, life and salvation to a liberated Algeria.

'Where have you been all this week?' his fellow missionaries enquired. It was at Bordj bou Arreridj a week later.

'I have been working in Algiers on the New Testament.'

'That is virtually impossible for no one has been allowed to go to Algiers all this week. No one got through the day that you went.'

'Where were they turned back?'

'At Menerville.' It was the very place, the only place where his papers had not been examined, not even asked for! Can any one doubt the power, wisdom and love of our God? There is nothing too hard for God.

Conditions at Lafayette became ever more severe. The whole village was surrounded with barbed-wire entanglements. There were more and more restrictions. Men were afraid to visit the mission house. The translations were almost completed. There had been a series of knockdown blows. It was then that an invitation to visit the Chad Republic, with a view to helping in the evangelisation of Muslims in that land, opened up a fresh avenue of service. To pack up their belongings and leave the home where their children had been born meant a real sacrifice. Yet the door in Algeria was closed for any effective work among men. In the Lord's mercy it could be opened widely again, but the time of waiting could be used profitably for God's glory. Abd alMasih and Lalla Jouhra went to Chad.

Having spent two years in the Chad, Abd alMasih and Lalla Jouhra returned to Lafayette to see if the door was once more open. They had left a man and his family to occupy the house and act as caretaker. An officer of the Algerian Army of Liberation had forcibly occupied the house, after obtaining the keys from a missionary under duress. Soon after he went in he threatened to kill the caretaker. To save his life he fled leaving the Algerian officer in complete control. He had taken over the whole of the house, and let the Hall to others. Many things had been stolen, and everywhere was filthy. He had refused to pay rent and rates, or for supplies of electricity. Abd alMasih and Lalla Jouhra informed the local official of their desire to return and recommence their work for the Lord. On hearing this the occupant of their home informed them that if anyone dared to set foot on the property, to come to meetings or classes, he would not hesitate, but would take his tommy-gun and use it. He had been responsible for the death of scores of innocent people in the area, and there is little doubt that had they returned he would have carried out his threat. This time it was the lives of others that were endangered and not their own. The Sub-Prefect asked them not to spend a single night in their own home, as he could not answer for the consequences if they did.

In order to show this cruel, godless man that he did not fear him, Abd alMasih returned to the house on a later occasion and spent two nights with him there alone. He was not afraid of him, but when the lives of others were threatened it was another matter. Finally, the man purchased the property for a nominal sum. It was sold to him under duress. The blow was severe, and the cost to them was . . . their home. The Lord later dealt with him as He does with all who rebel against Him, and for years he was an object of pity and scorn. 'There goes the man who attempted to stop God's work,' they said.

For the time being the work of Abd alMasih and Lalla Jouhra in Algeria was complete and they left for Central Africa to translate yet another New Testament, and to supply precision tools such as tracts, a hymn book and an approach course for African evangelists. Once again God had opened to them a large field of service.

Looking back they can trace God's hand in it all. The successive blows were hard to bear; the last blow was the hardest of all, especially for Lalla Jouhra. Each blow had proved a knock-down, but not a knockout, and each setback resulted in a larger sphere of service. These successive blows made 2 Corinthians 4: 6–18 more precious. This is God's way of working. If you, dear reader, have just had a knock-down blow, do not let it be a knockout blow, as the enemy intends, but get up and fight on. The battle is the Lord's. He will vindicate you and manifest His power to save, as the sequel of this story shows.

Chapter Fifteen

Dawning – A New Era

In 1962, amid scenes of wild rejoicing, the long seven-year war came to an end and Algeria was granted independence. To save their lives over a million Europeans left the country, most of them abandoning their homes, furniture and all that they possessed. The European churches and assemblies ceased to exist. Many people were convinced that when independence came all Christian work would automatically cease, but, true to their promises, the Algerian authorities granted religious liberty to the very small Christian minority, and God's work continued. Alas, this impartial attitude was maintained only for a few years, but all can rejoice that during that period there was an evident working of the Holy Spirit in the lives of many young people. God has said, 'I work and who can hinder it?' (Is. 43:13). There is nothing too hard for God.

Their work of translation in the Chad was finished and Abd alMasih and Lalla Jouhra returned to Algeria in 1967, and for several months lived again in a Kabyle village. It was very obvious that, in places in the interior of the country where the gospel had been proclaimed for many years and the people were hardened because of their refusal to obey, God was no longer working, except among the children and young people. The people appreciated the social services rendered by the missionary, and were most friendly, but any attempt on the part of a younger person to break with Islam was persistently opposed by all. Indeed, many elderly Kabyles insisted that they did believe in the Lord Jesus, but they persisted in observing the fast of Ramadhan, and some even prayed in the mosques. Others asserted that they really were Christians, but that Jesus did not die. It became more and more evident that these people had heard and refused. Missionaries were courageously and faithfully continuing their service for God, but one by one the Mission stations of the interior were closing. In striking contrast a more liberal spirit prevailed in the towns. Friday prayers in the mosques were well attended, but Islam was losing its grip on the younger generation. In an effort to bring them back, the Koran was being taught in all schools, and in many schools all the lessons were in Arabic. In the towns God had begun a new work. In the spiritual realm a new day had dawned.

Abd alMasih faced the biggest challenge of his life. Now an old man of sixty-eight, he had been invited to be padre to a mixed camp of teenagers in independent Algeria. Every one of the group of sixty was from a Muslim family. He looked into the faces of these keen young people as they gathered under the pine trees, close to the Mediterranean sea. Fifty yards away was a holiday camp run by Algerians for their children. They were singing worldly Muslim songs and their voices came across on the night air. Here before him were strapping young men, taller than himself, some of them convinced Muslims, others out for fun and a good time. Light, flippant girls mingled with their more serious sisters. He had to be responsible for passing on over forty messages during the next three weeks, and he was answerable to God for their souls. He faced an impossible task. Prayer was the only answer.

'Will any keen Algerian Christians who would like to join me in prayer please come to my small hut this evening?' He expected, he hoped, that two, or perhaps three would come. Thirty-two turned up! They sat on the bed, on the table, on the form and stood two deep round the walls. 'If you ask . . . I will do,' was the promise. They did ask, and God worked so that in that one camp twenty-one Muslims trusted the Saviour. How wonderful in any land, but in independent Algeria!

But why a mixed camp in a land where girls are shut away? Missionaries have an important part to play in the emancipation of girls and women. Only through the gospel can these girls find true freedom. Immorality is the problem in every country today. In a land where girls are confined to their homes at the age of puberty a moral re-education is essential. The sexes must mix, but in a Christian atmosphere, where the moral interests of the girls will be safeguarded. These girls are the future mothers and, if Christian homes can be formed where the children will be brought up in the fear of the Lord, the possibilities are tremendous. So Algerian parents are willing for their daughters to attend camps where God's Word is taught, because of the healthy moral atmosphere.

Zeena was a bright vivacious girl of thirteen. Her deep-throated voice contrasted strangely with her white complexion and rosy cheeks. She was determined to resist all spiritual teaching. She had come to camp to enjoy herself; the bathing, the games, the sing-songs, the good food, plenty of boys, appealed to her immensely; so she would enjoy them, and do her best to stop anyone listening to the Word of God. She sat at the back of the meeting laughing with her companions, giggling, making fun of the message, pulling the hair of the girl in front. The Holy Spirit was at work in that camp. The message of the previous

evening had not been forgotten. There had been no appeal
to raise hands, no playing on the emotions. The message
having been given, there were a few moments of prayer,
and then they went to bed. That message still rang in her
ears the next day. By the time afternoon came she could
stand it no longer. Someone must help her with this battle,
this turmoil in her heart. She confided to the leader, 'I have
been a naughty girl. I have done wrong.' She was in tears.
The leader was shocked. 'Surely you have not got into
trouble with a boy?' 'No, worse than that. I have sinned
against Jesus. I have said "No" to Him.' As she knelt in
prayer, between her sobs, she said, 'Lord Jesus, I came to
this camp determined not to listen. I did not want to listen.
I did not want You, and I tried to stop others. Yet You died
for me. Please forgive me, Lord. Please forgive.' He did.

Khalidja was a timid girl of fourteen. She had two
friends who were radiant Christians, and they were trying to win her for Christ. To them she confided that she
really did want to believe, but she was so afraid of her
Dad. 'He will whip me and beat me, if ever I become a
Christian.' The day came when she could hold out no
longer. Just after dinner she went along with her two
friends, and very simply, yet very sincerely, committed
her life to Him Who is able to save. Then she went off to
siesta during the heat of the day. At 3 o'clock she was
back at the padre's hut. 'Uncle,' she said. 'I went right off
to sleep and I had a vivid dream. A horrid man came to
me.' She described the man, a man with diabolical looks.
'He said to me, "Khalidja, what have you done? You have
left your religion to follow Jesus. I will never, never leave
you until I kill you, or until you come back to Islam, and
if you don't I shall do this, and that . . . You will suffer
unspeakably. You will be beaten and starved." Who was
he, Uncle?' she asked, 'What does it mean?' She was terrified. Abd alMasih could only tell her that the devil

himself was trying to turn her aside from allegiance to Christ.

Later in the afternoon her two girl friends came along and with tears in their eyes, said, 'Khalidja has denied the Lord. She told the other girls that she really did not mean it. She was not sincere.' There was only one resort: prayer. The two girls remained after the prayer meeting that evening to pray for Khalidja. Each of them prayed, and then Abd alMasih committed her to the Lord. He thought that they would immediately join the others at games, but they each prayed again, and yet again. Seldom are such prayers heard, and when they come from hearts that only a year before were in bondage to Islam they are full of the music of heaven. 'Lord, show Yourself to Khalidja, in all Your magnificence, in all Your power and glory, in all Your beauty and strength. Lord, Satan has shown his hand. If she only sees You, Lord Jesus, she will never go back.' Or again, 'Lord, You have said; "No man shall pluck them out of My hand." Hold her fast, Lord!'

Thus these two radiant Christians pleaded for their friend. Three days later she again committed her life to the Lord Jesus. She knew that her father would give her a beating when he heard that she was a Christian, but with tremendous courage she went to face it.

Every morning the whole group gathered to study the book of Exodus and the story of redemption. Then they went to the beach for bathing and games. In the evening a simple gospel message was given in Arabic or French. Then there was a brief time of quiet when each one was invited to consider the claims of the Redeemer before going to bed. During the following day those who had surrendered their lives to the Saviour, or who desired spiritual help came along for a quiet talk.

It was Sunday evening. In a clearing of the forest the camp fire burned brightly. A young fellow of seventeen gave his testimony. 'God greatly blessed me when I came to camp last year and I trusted the Saviour. I went back home and met with terrible opposition. They tore my Bible to pieces, they hit me and cursed me. I went down into the depths of despair. Everything was black. My faith went. But God in His grace has spoken to me again this year. I have been greatly helped and blessed. I am going back home to follow Him all the way. It may mean that they will turn me out of home. I know they will oppose me. Perhaps they will try and poison me. Pray for me that God may keep me true.' God graciously helped him to stand and the following year he returned as a camp monitor. By his steadfast loyalty, his self-discipline, his solid spirituality during a period of six weeks of intensive effort, he proved himself a stalwart servant of God.

It is obvious that the great test for these young converts comes when they face their families.

Miriam was sixteen. She had thanked the Lord for opening His great heart of love and taking her in. Now she faced the crucial test. They were driving through the town and approaching her home. She was returning as a Christian. The van drew up. She seized her case, and without a word she scuttled off like a frightened rabbit. Not a word of thanks. Not even 'Goodbye'. Was she real? Would she stand? That same evening she went to the little Mission Hall with her younger sister, who was leaving for the next camp. Her mother, brothers and sisters and aunt were with her. The aunt had never before entered a Mission Hall, but seeing the organ, she said, 'Oh, a dance hall. Let's have a dance,' and sat down to play! Abd alMasih thought that it was time for him to intervene. He played one of the camp choruses, 'He was nailed to the Cross for me.'

Having finished, he proceeded to play another, but Miriam had come up behind and joined in the singing. She wanted to sing the whole hymn. Her clear girlish voice rang out, 'What a wonderful Saviour I have. He sacrificed Himself for me, and He gave His innocent life to die on that cruel cross. He was nailed to the Cross for me.' Thus she took her stand before her mother and the mocking aunt. The hardest step for any convert from Islam is to tell the family circle. Having done this what a transformation took place in Miriam! The timid girl of the morning became a bright witness for the Lord, full of His joy. Miriam has gone on with the Lord. She resisted several attempts to make her marry a Muslim, but finally has been forced to do so against her will. Nothing is too hard for God, and it may well be that she will win her husband for Christ.

Wherever there is a work of God Satan will challenge it and attempt to hinder. As the confidence of the young Muslims was won, they felt able to express their doubts and their difficulties. Question time revealed what was in some minds.

A very keen Christian lad of seventeen said to Abd alMasih, 'Uncle, I want to answer two of those questions. They will listen to me, perhaps more than to you, for I was a Muslim and am now a Christian.' He gave some excellent answers to his friends, from the Scriptures.

The lad who asked most of the questions was the son of an ardent nationalist who had been killed in the war. This boy later wrote, 'I went away from that camp feeling physically ill. I could not forget the messages from the Word of God, the daily Bible studies. I remembered the faithful way in which we were told of sins that we did not even know were sin, the warm earnestness with which our salvation from hell was sought, and, above all, the prayers of the Algerian Christians. God worked in my heart, and NOW I AM SAVED I want everyone to know it.' What a triumph of grace in the heart of this Saul of Tarsus, that, four months after leaving the camp, he was saved!

The opposition was even more pronounced during the camp for adolescents the following year. Once again over sixty teenagers had gathered, mostly those of the fifteen-to-sixteen age group. This time the leaders and co-leaders of each group were Christians from Muslim homes. They themselves were only a year or two older than the young people for whom they were responsible. How wonderful to find Algerian Christians willing to spend their holidays in winning others for the Lord!

The pattern was very similar to the previous year. Studies on Genesis every morning, group studies on various Scriptures in the afternoon, and a gospel message each evening. Some of these messages were given by the young Algerians. They also conducted the revision of the previous day's lesson. Family prayers were in their hands, and during the camp each of these young workers was called on to give his or her testimony to the saving grace of God in Jesus Christ.

'To whom might the Lord have referred when He said, "beware of false prophets"? '

This rather provocative question was put to the groups for individual and collective study. The leader of each studygroup, a camper, was to give the collective answer for the group. The girls' group began. 'Seventh Day Adventists,' said the first group. 'Jehovah's Witnesses,' said the second. 'Mohammed,' said the third. Abd alMasih hastened on to the answers from the boys' groups, deliberately turning a deaf ear to the murmurs of disapproval coming from some of the campers. It is best to ignore such a frontal attack, even when it comes from a

Christian group of former Muslims. Then the voice of a keen Algerian boy was heard. 'Uncle, did you not notice the reaction to one reply? It is obvious that there are some here who do not agree that Mohammed is a false prophet. I should like to prove to them from the Scriptures that he was.' He proceeded to do so.

Immediately there was a sharp division in the camp. It was now evident to all that no one can profess to believe in the Lord Jesus and maintain a secret allegiance to Mohammed. The girl who had read out the findings of her group was told that she ought to be ashamed, and that she deserved to be killed. Another boy started to sing a deliberate untruth in parody of a Christian chorus. 'I am so glad that Mohammed saved me.' The poor lad was fully aware that Mohammed had not, and could not save him, but he felt that he must give expression to his feelings. On returning from the Sunday walk a message was found written on the dining room table, 'You are all hidebound, and do not know what you are talking about. You do not believe in Jesus or Mohammed.' It was quite obvious that a crisis had been reached. It could be met only by prayer. Abd alMasih's little room was packed to capacity when the young Christians met for prayer that evening. Elsewhere the Algerian leaders had gathered to pray.

Two days later, when all signs of the rebellious spirit had passed, Abd alMasih had a quiet talk with each of the ringleaders, and especially with the lad who had written the insulting message. It was not easy to continue the gospel messages in such an atmosphere, but the impact was even more direct. No reference was ever made to the Prophet of Islam, but the question box was in continual use. From a Christian girl came the challenge, 'Will any Muslim come forward and in five minutes tell us any one thing Mohammed has done for him, that Jesus Christ has not done for us.' No one volunteered to attempt to do so.

From Muslims came, 'Why does the Koran speak of Jesus Christ, and the Bible does not mention Mohammed?' and 'How can we know that the Bible speaks the truth?'

It was now evident that God was working in some lives. The fellows who were so opposed followed the messages even more closely. Zeetonia had been sent to camp at the very last minute. Her brother had returned from the previous camp and had evidently given such a glowing account to his mother that late that evening she rang up to know if her daughter could attend the last camp. The train left at 6.30 the next morning, and it left with Zeetonia aboard. Never before had she been under Christian ministry. She opened up as a flower to the sun as she listened to the wonderful message of the gospel. Not a word was missed. On the fifth day of camp she asked for prayer, and the next day told everyone that she had trusted the Lord Jesus as her Saviour. It was wonderful to see the spiritual growth of this fifteen-year-old girl. She was soon put in touch with a keen Christian girl of her own age, and day after day they could be seen walking together, engaged in serious conversation about their problems, and the solution from the Word of God. To hear this babe in Christ pour out her heart in prayer was music indeed. One would have thought her an experienced Christian. Her spiritual insight was soon evident to all. Yes, God was working and day after day these young people came, until sixteen had professed conversion, ten girls and six fellows.

In several families three or four trusted the Saviour. It was evident that God was answering their prayers for Christian families. By the second week it was obvious that there were more Christians than Muslims and so the messages of the last four days were designed to help the Lord's own. They were taught the truths of the Lordship of Christ, discipleship and practical sanctification.

The last evening had come and all were seated around

the camp fire for the final messages. Several of the testimonies were outstanding in their appeal, as one after another told of a new-found life in Christ. By the light of the fire Abd alMasih stood to give his final message, 'All day long I have stretched forth my hands to a disobedient and gainsaying people.' No appeal was made, but all were aware that this was the last opportunity for some. All were to rise at 4.30 the next morning for the long journey back to the towns. God's servant closed in prayer, but as he turned away from the circle, a tall figure approached. It was the ringleader of the Muslims, the fellow who had written the insulting message. He had come to say 'Goodbye'. As he kissed Abd alMasih on both cheeks, the servant of God said to him, 'So you are leaving having made no decision?' 'I have made my decision,' was the quiet reply. 'I have come to Christ.' Having read the Scriptures together, they knelt in prayer and the little hut was the scene of deep repentance, as the erstwhile fanatical Muslim told the Saviour that he surrendered unconditionally to Him and accepted Him as Saviour and Lord.

The burned out hulk of a bus

Every isolated farmhouse was destroyed

Chapter Sixteen

Victory is Sure

'Lord, there are some people who say that it is impossible for a Muslim to be converted and to become a Christian. That there will never again be Christian churches in this Muslim land. But, Lord, You can see that all of us here this evening are from Muslim homes. We love You, we believe in You. We are the tangible evidence that You can save Muslims. You have saved us. We are here as members of Your Church, the first of many who will believe in You in this land. We are the pioneers of the new churches in Algeria. Lord, we are the proof that the devil lies. Lord, go on to do a deep work in us and through us everywhere in this land.'

There were fervent 'Amens,' as this young Christian closed his prayer. Forty-five young Algerians bowed in prayer beneath the trees. Fellows and girls sat on the carpet of pine needles in a large circle as the darkness fell, and one after another they poured out their hearts to God in the above strain, sharing in fervent, earnest prayer. Their evening meal over, they were at liberty to amuse themselves in this Bible-study camp, but instead they chose each evening to gather for prayer. The prayers continued.

'Lord, save our parents. We know that You want to save whole families. It is written, "believe on the Lord Jesus Christ and you shalt be saved, and your house". Lord, we are the first in our families to believe. Lord, how wonderful it would be to have a Christian home! A home where we could sit and quietly read Your Word every day without having it snatched from our hands or having pages torn out. A home where we could quietly pray without interference, where we could openly sing these lovely hymns and choruses whenever we wanted to, instead of being cursed and shouted at and hit. A home where we could find sympathy and love, and not opposition and blows. Lord, save our families, and give us Christian homes.'

There were no long prayers. Nearly everyone present prayed, and the burden of each was that, when they returned to their homes, God would keep them faithful in the face of the continual and severe opposition. That He would strengthen the girls who had been beaten when they returned from a previous camp and informed their parents that they were now Christians.

'Lord, make me to desire joyfully Your will, and give me the strength to do it.'

Abd alMasih bowed his head in humble worship and adoration as he listened to these fervent prayers. Here, indeed, was concrete evidence that nothing is too hard for God. This was what he had prayed for, the aim of his labours for so many years. A band of over fifty Christian young people in this Muslim land.

A challenge had come to Abd alMasih as soon as he arrived at this camp. The fifty young Algerians were of both sexes, and their ages ranged from fourteen to twenty-three. For the next fortnight they were to mix freely together, in a land where girls and women have always been segregated. He was asked to give this mixed company a straight talk on morality and sex ethics. But to speak of sex in a public meeting in Algeria is absolutely taboo. To mention the word 'adultery' in a village meeting in Kabylia is to lose the entire audience of men. It was a man very much cast on God who gave that opening message. Yet, under God, it paved the way for what followed. In this time of transition, of breaking with past traditions, both girls and fellows are faced with many problems. In an amazing way these young people confided in the ageing servant of God.

'Is it wrong for a girl to think of marriage?'

'What sort of a girl should a fellow choose in a country where the girl is not chosen for him?'

'Can a Christian girl marry a Muslim?'

'What if she should be compelled to do so?'

'Should a Christian girl go to a Muslim wedding, and put on the henna dye?'

Fatima is Kabyle. She is a missionary and has three children. To Abd alMasih she confided, 'It is wonderful to see the way you have so quickly won the confidence of these young people. They talk to you as if you were their father: more than that, for they would not dare to speak of some of these things with their own parents. How do you do it?'

He found the answer to her question in Paul's plea to the Galatians, 'Become as I am, for I am as you are.' To his fellow workers he confided, 'If we want these young people to become like us in Christian faith and doctrine, we must become like them putting ourselves in their place in Christian sympathy and love. We must share their problems, suffering with them, giving them the benefit of our knowledge of the Scriptures and experience of God's faithfulness.' Such work is costly, and Abd alMasih's pillow was often wet with tears as during the night he battled with the problems of these dear young Christians who are faced with continual ostracism and opposition in their homes. He had faced stones, danger and opposition for Christ's sake, and through the years God had delivered him but he had always been able to return to the love and sympathy of his helpmeet and the shelter of a Christian home. But for these young people there could be no withdrawal. The opposition was sustained and continual. Yet he did not hesitate to give them the true Scriptural answer. There could be no divided loyalties. Christ must be Lord. The cost of discipleship was high, the world must be renounced, and self crucified. The teaching of the Galatian epistle which they were studying left no room for choice. A visitor from France was overheard to say, 'Never before have we heard the truths of discipleship, of Christian discipline and of fidelity to Christ, at whatever cost, so plainly taught. Yet they take it, for all he says is with such love, that they listen, count the cost, accept, and are prepared to follow their Lord . . . all the way.'

For an hour and a half each morning they studied the epistle to the Galatians and found that the teaching completely fitted their spiritual needs. Later each day they separated into six groups for a closer study of the daily passage. Each student had to write down the answer to five questions based on the Scripture text, then the answers were written down by the group leader, and finally the whole camp shared them. Their deep exercise of heart was evident from their continual questions.

'Is it a sin for a Christian to observe the Fast of Ramadhan?'

'If our parents compel us to fast what should we do? Obey our parents, and go against our conscience or . . .?'

'Should we eat the meat of the sacrifice offered at the Feast of Sheep?'

'What must one do when one has sinned inadvertently, or through ignorance?'

Independent witness to the changed lives of some of these young people was given later in a letter from a Salvation Army officer to a friend.

'Dalmabiya has completely changed. It is a pleasure to see the way in which she is opening up. Rahma must accept marriage to a Muslim or be turned from home. She refuses. They came to arrange a marriage for Zeineb, but she refuses. She declares, "I am a Christian. I will NEVER marry a Muslim." Halima has brought me her Bible. Her brother wants to burn it. Truly the devil is mad with rage. A good sign, but these poor young people!'

Rahma was asked by her schoolteacher to pray Muslim prayers. She refused and was caned before the whole class.

The Lord took Abd alKader from the camp to a desert oasis, where he is the only Christian. Converted a year ago he has made tremendous strides in his spiritual life and is able to give a clear message from the Word. Has the Lord taken him to the desert to form another Paul for Algeria?

Sadik came to the Lord in the camp a year ago. A lad of seventeen, he was often seen with his open Bible talking to one or two Muslim men, seeking ardently to win them for Christ.

Yamina trusted the Lord as Saviour during the camp and returned to her home to find that her parents were not opposed. She had many problems. Should she cut herself off completely from her family and worldly friends? The test came when she was invited to go to the women's baths with a girlfriend who was about to be married. She knew the time there would be a time of merriment, when dancing and some rather lewd practices would be observed. She prayed and felt that the Lord would have her go. Acutely aware of her position as a Christian, she withdrew from her friends, who approached her and asked why she was no longer one with them. Her confession of Christ as her Lord involved her in scorn, ridicule and suffering. As she looked on the misconduct of her friends, her own heart was deeply moved in gratitude to the One who had saved her from such practices, and the tears quietly flowed down her cheeks. Another friend approached her with a taunt,

'It is obvious that you are unhappy because you are no longer with us. Come on in.' To which she replied, 'I am not weeping because I am unhappy. On the contrary, I have a deep inward joy of which you know nothing, the joy and peace that only God can give. I am weeping as I see the excesses to which you commit yourselves.' The friend left her to continue her merriment with her Muslim sisters, but ten minutes later she came and beckoned to Yamina to follow her outside. When they were alone she said, 'I want you to tell me how I can find the peace and joy that you have.' Yamina produced her Bible and pointed her to the Lord Jesus.

'Can I borrow this wonderful Book?' said her friend. That night she went round to Yamina's house and accepted the Lord Jesus as her Saviour. She told her friends, and four others now study the Word of God each evening.

Fereeda was in revolt against God. She had asked God time and again to incline her parents to consent to her becoming a Christian, but they had refused. She had prayed so hard, so intently, but there seemed no answer. She had done her best to become a Christian, but it was useless to try to be a Christian where she lived. Her deep resentment and deep-seated rebellion were evident on her face. It was useless to argue with her. But the Lord triumphed in her life. She surrendered to Christ and a few days after returning home she wrote to her friend, 'I wanted to tell mother, and on July 30th God gave me the courage to do so. I told her how the Lord Jesus had saved me. She reproached me bitterly. She shouts at me whenever she sees me reading my Bible. When I spoke to her about the Lord Jesus she grew mad with anger, and treated me as a *kafra* (a heathen girl). She told me to go, as I must no longer remain with her in the same house. She said, "I don't want to remain in the same house with you when you have changed your religion." I told her that the Lord Jesus is the only Way to God, and that He alone gave Himself for our sins. She hit me again and again. She invited me to repent and return to Islam. I told her that every Muslim is under law, and therefore condemned. If he does not accept Jesus as his personal Saviour he will remain under the condemnation of God. I told mother that I could no longer conscientiously observe the Fast of Ramadhan as it forms part of a religion of works; only if compelled to do so would I fast. But she does not understand. "You were born Muslim and you will remain Muslim," she says. I beg you to pray for me. Pray that my mother will understand, and that I may be able to convince her from the Word of God. Pray that God will strengthen me in the faith in spite of all the wrongs that have been done to me.'

A letter written to Abd alMasih a fortnight later showed she was experiencing the keeping power of God. She wrote, 'My mother is unchanged. She now seeks to persuade me to be a Christian in secret, without telling anyone of my faith, but that is impossible. She went to the mosque for Friday prayers. The *imam* (religious leader) spoke to them of the Lord Jesus and the miracles that He performed. She told me "We believe in the Lord Jesus, but our religion is purer than yours." Mother now tries to persuade me by speaking to me kindly, but all I know is that a Christian girl who has pledged herself to follow the Lord Jesus, must never, no never, turn back. It was very hard to endure all the difficulties and hardships during the first days. I asked the Lord to help me, and I can say that until now He has always answered my prayers. Even though the persecution has not stopped, He has given me the courage to bear it.'

Areski told his fellow Christians in the following terms of the opposition that he had faced for Christ's sake.

'That day I went home and told my parents that I believed in the Lord Jesus Christ as my Saviour. I told them of my peace of heart, and of my assurance of salvation. They replied: "Then you are no longer an Algerian. You have not only renounced your faith, but you are a traitor to your country." They deprived me of food for many days, and that is hard for a growing boy. Then my mother refused to do my washing for weeks on end. "If you are a Christian, then you can go dirty, for you are no longer my son." For a long time no one in my home spoke to me. They told me that if I still persisted in following the Lord Jesus, they would poison me. Then they put me on the street. Yes, I was turned from home and the dear ones I loved. They took me back and made me go before the religious leaders. All the big imams did their best to turn me from the Lord. They beat me. They threatened me with death. They tried to force me to repeat Muslim prayers. Then they changed their tactics, and tried to coax me back to Islam by offering all the advantages of their religion, and inducements of the flesh. I was able to refute everything they said from their own Koran and from the Word of God. They could give me no proof that Mohammed is superior to my Lord. You all know how the severe test comes round each year at the Fast of Ramadhan. They did their best to make me fast. My friends laugh at me, and make fun of me, but by the grace of God I have stood firm. The hardest of all is when my mother reproaches me for being a Christian. I have to bear this continually. She says "You have betrayed me. For nine months I suffered for your sake, when I carried you ... I suffered to give you life.

I cared for you when you were a baby. Many, many times I have denied myself in order to give to you, and now you turn against me and betray my love. You have betrayed your country, your family, and me your mother." My friends, I can tell you that my mother's continual tears and pleading are enough to break my heart. It is worse than all the blows, worse than the hunger and the threats. Yet, I cannot go back and deny my Lord, even for the sake of my mother.'

The question is often asked, 'Do these converts stand? Do they go on?' Some go on well for a time, and then are turned aside by the continual opposition and persecution. In fact there are very few who do not at some time draw back in the face of the fierce opposition, but the true child of God invariably returns to Him. Merzouga was very keen for the Lord. She returned from the camps to face ostracism and opposition. Her brother beat her day after day and threatened to kill her if she did not renounce her faith in Christ. She went to work in a Muslim hospital and lost her love for the Lord. She even turned against other Christians and denounced them. Fervent prayer went up on her behalf and, although unable to return to the camps, she did come back to the Lord. Abd alMasih was impressed by this phrase in her prayer, 'Lord, give me back that ardour, that audacity that I once had to speak to others of You in the face of opposition.' This hit him hard. How little do we know of that ardour which witnesses for Christ in the face of continual ostracism and persecution! Yet these young Christians do just that. They seize every opportunity to witness for their Lord.

Many Christians are distressed by recent news from Algeria. The enemy of souls is determined to undermine and destroy the work of God in that land. Workers are expelled, Christians are tracked down, threatened, intimidated and persecuted. Details of the severe sufferings of God's people cannot be given, even when known, but Algeria is quickly becoming a closed land. Yet there is positive evidence that God is building His Church, and it is impossible for the power of darkness to overcome it. God has been pleased to close the door to much foreign missionary work. He shuts and no man can open. He opens and no man shuts.

> 'The Lord is King, who then shall dare
> Resist His will, distrust His care,
> Or murmur at His wise decrees,
> Or doubt His royal promises?'

The foreigners leave, but the work of God continues. The promises hold. Final victory is sure.

Communications with suffering Christians may cease as letters are intercepted. The only way to help these brave, privileged men and women is by prayer. Persecution may drive them underground, but God will triumph. To them it is given not only to believe in Christ's name, but also to suffer for His sake. What a glorious crown will be theirs when the Lord returns!

Throughout the world today God is working among Muslims. As one door closes we must be prepared to enter others that are open, if not as full-time missionaries, then in other ways.

The new Algeria

'... Shall doubtless come again with rejoicing, bringing his sheaves'

Chapter Seventeen

Nothing Too Hard For God

'Sir, we are delighted to know that Algerian Christians will be given the same liberty as Muslims in the New Algeria. Does this also mean that a Muslim will be free to change his faith and become Christian?' asked the missionary.

'Such a thing is unthinkable,' was the unequivocal reply from the high Muslim official. To the unbeliever it is not only impossible for a Muslim to become a Christian, it is beyond the wildest bounds of imagination. Yet God is Almighty. There is nothing too hard for the living God.

It was the closing night of the camp for Bible study. The campfire was burning and several Algerian Christians had given striking evidence of the way in which Christ had transformed their lives. Then a young man of eighteen, speaking from a full heart, and with deep emotion as he referred to his parents, tried to prepare his fellow countrymen for the fiery trial that awaited them when they returned to their homes. Unhappily his words lose some of their power by translation.

'God is powerful. I should like to say that to those fellows and girls who have accepted Christ in this camp, and who are now about to return to their homes. I accepted Christ into my heart, but it was a considerable time before

I told my parents. I am sure that I did wrong in not telling them before. Really, the people whom we should love and cherish more than anyone else in the world are our parents. If we desire to speak of Christ to our friends, we must speak to our parents first of all. I myself hesitated to do this because I was afraid. Why was I afraid? I was afraid, that's all. But God wanted me to speak to my parents and it was God who decided that I should do so. I was forced to do it. One day I was faced with the choice. I could not go back. Either I could deny my faith in Christ, or I could confess Him. Only these two ways were open to me. I should like to tell you what happened afterwards. I do not want to say this to boast in any way, or to say to you, "Look, this is what I did." No, but just to prove to you the power of God in an Algerian Christian. People have a tendency to say – and even Christian leaders say it – that a Muslim can never become a Christian. I say, "I was a Muslim and now I am a Christian." I should like to say what God can do in a Muslim who becomes a Christian. When you confess Christ, of course, your family no longer speaks to you. After that they no longer give you food, or do your washing. That is not enough. The next thing is the mosque, and you will be called before the Imams. Some of them will ply you with questions with a certain psychology, others will be more brutal . . . But what is hardest of all to bear is the impression that one has of having betrayed a mother's love, a father's love. Several times I have cried in front of my mother when she told me all that she had suffered for my sake . . . That impression that one has of having betrayed her love. That is what chokes you. It is terrible in the extreme. Something that you just cannot bear. You feel so small. You feel such a terrible sadness that you just want to disappear altogether. Then it is that God shows His love. That is when He shows His power. Over and over again I have been tempted to say to my mother, just to please her

(Yes, I know that this is very superficial), that I was no longer a Christian. But God was always there. He always arranged everything for the best. He gave me strength to go on with Christ. Several times I have been in the hands of the Imams in a mosque, and there they used the Koran; they tried logic, showing how in a Muslim land it is much easier to follow what the Koran says as it is the Word of God. I reached the utmost limit, really it was the limit. I was on the point of doubting what I had seen in the light. But God gave me the answers and delivered me. I want to say this to you my friends, "You must never doubt in the darkness what you have seen in the light." In this camp you have seen that the Bible is the Word of God. You are going home, and I am sure that in one way or another you will be tempted to your utmost limits to doubt the Word of God. Satan is powerful, he is the prince of this world, but he is not almighty. You know in your hearts that Christ is the Saviour, and you will go back home and by every means in their power they will try and turn you back. But I plead with you, try and come back to all that you have learned in this camp, that Christ is the only Saviour and the Bible the Word of God. Never doubt in the darkness what you have learned in the light, and Christ will bless you and He will give you strength. He will make it possible for you to triumph in every trial and temptation. I say this because this is what happened to me, and God has shown his power through me. I would never have thought that I could have stood against the Imams, as I did, with all their books, but by the POWER OF GOD and, all glory to Him, that is what happened.'

There were many who said, 'Praise the Lord!' from the depth of their hearts as he sat down. There is nothing too hard for God. He not only saves, but He is able to keep His children. Men may even kill the body but they cannot touch the life which is hid with Christ in God.

'Dad, did you know that at camp Nuwara's group said that Mohammed is a false prophet?'

Nuwara was sitting at table with her brother and sister, her mother and father. When he heard this, her father was almost beside himself. In fury he turned to his seventeen-year-old daughter and said, 'I hope that you had nothing to do with this?' Calmly she replied, 'Father, I was the only one in the group to make the statement.' His fury knew no bounds. He took Nuwara into the next room, and thrashed her for at least ten minutes. The next day he told her, 'You had better go to your Grandmother's house. I don't ever want to see you again. All my love for you has gone.' How easy it would have been for Nuwara to have remained silent, to hide her light, to deny the words in order to escape that cruel beating, the shame and the suffering! She later wrote to Abd alMasih,

'Dear Uncle, forgive this delay in writing. I chose not to write before, for I wanted to be sure just what was going to happen. I told my father that I was a Christian, but he did not take me seriously. He laughed it off. Then my brother told what I had said about Mohammed . . . You cannot imagine how unhappy I was after Father had beaten me and had said those cruel words. I was on the point of turning back, and giving up. Then I remembered that you told me that, with my strong character, God wanted me to be a leader. His servant . . . I pray daily for the Christians of Algeria. Dear Uncle, you know that I am deeply grieved to see people all round me dying without forgiveness and without being ready to die. I long to see the church of Jesus Christ established here in Algeria. Then all Algerians could perhaps hear the gospel and find the way of salvation. That is my daily prayer. I always carry the New Testament with me in my satchel and I have been able to lead two other girls to the Saviour. Their names are . . . and . . . They will soon be writing to tell you.'

Later Nuwara was able to write to a friend,

'I am so glad to tell you that my parents are no longer persecuting me as they did. I believe that this is a miracle wrought by the Lord. Latterly I have read my Bible a lot, and I am dazzled and fascinated by the power and the richness of the promises. Each morning I feel that I simply must thank the Great Giver of all good Whom I adore. The more I read the Bible, the more I discover that Christ is too good for us, for we do not deserve all this. . . . He suffered for us. Did Mohammed do this? No. That's what I tell all my friends, who think that I am ridiculous. I want to tell you something which may make you laugh. I should so much like to die for Christ, in order to say "Thank you" to Him. Of course it is hard to think this, but when I reflect on all He has done for me. . . !'

A few weeks later Abd alMasih received another letter from her from which extracts only can be given.

'Dear Uncle, I have tremendous news for you which will certainly give you much pleasure. Part of my prayers have been answered. I knew that a miracle was about to happen . . . Every afternoon we come together for a meeting . . . We pray together, read and sing. I do my best to explain a passage of Scripture. It's wonderful! Now I am coming to the surprise. One day my mother came up and she heard us singing. She came in, took a spare chair and listened to the end. Then I switched over and explained the passage in Arabic. She was really touched, and since then she has never missed one of these meetings. I am sure that Christ is working in her heart to the full. She has told me that promises given to Christians are so wonderful and beautiful that she wants to hook on to them. So I have understood many things . . . Ever since I do not cease to thank the Lord for His help, for I feel that He is with me. I want you to give me some advice, and some ideas so that I know what to say during these little meetings. I find that it is really quite hard.'

Thus in widely separated towns God has His witnesses who, in the face of opposition, are winning others to a living faith in Christ. The choice for them is clear. To hide their light, and remain secret disciples, or to be brave enough to confess their Lord, to stand firm, to suffer, and to win others for the Saviour.

'He that goeth forth and weepeth, bearing precious seed, shall doubtless come again with rejoicing, bringing his sheaves with him.' This was the reassuring verse that God had often brought to the mind of Abd alMasih over the years. There had been times when he had questioned if such a promise could hold good in Muslim lands. It is a three-fold promise with a three-fold condition. The Eastern sower goes forth leaving behind him the comforts of home and fireside. The season for sowing is limited. He cannot sow until the rains have prepared the ground, and he must complete his sowing before the snow falls. He sows in the face of bitter wind and sleet. Facing the wintry weather he recalls that the seed which he scatters has cost him a whole year of his life. It is costly, precious seed. He had sown seed the previous year, watched over it and weeded it, reaped it and threshed it, winnowed it and stored it. It is, indeed, costly seed. Much of it will be lost, but because of God's faithfulness there will be a harvest.

The Christian sower sows the Word of God. This three-fold condition must be observed continually and applied to his service. He must go forth. There must be a continual outreach, an extension of the field of sowing in spite of adverse conditions. Each message that he gives must cost him something. It must have been lived out in his life, have become a part of his life. It must be a message from God, received in the quietness of his room as he waits before God. He must be in close fellowship with his Lord Who wept in Gethsemane, who sobbed and wept over unrepentant Jerusalem. From a heart filled with deep compassion for men he must faithfully proclaim the message even to those who oppose and persecute.

Abd alMasih thought of the poem that he had pasted in the front of his Bible many years previously, a poem which had so often been an encouragement to him during the forty-five years of sowing with tears.

'I wanted to sow in a fertile field
That bordered a pleasant land,
Where fellowships sweet their joys would yield,
And comforts be mine to command.

He gave me instead, a barren spot
In a land that was wild and drear,
Where peril and hardship must be my lot –
Afar from all I held dear.

But I learned that the field of His choice was fair,
Far better than any beside,
For the Master, also, laboured there –
My Strength, my Companion and Guide.'

Abd alMasih thought of the long years of sowing, sometimes with bitter heartbreaks, the martyrdom of the first believers, the intense opposition, the bitter persecutions, the hope deferred that made the heart sick, the sufferings of the shut-in women, the repeated disappointments, the fellowship of His sufferings, the years of preparation of the precious Seed, the loss of successive outstations, and finally of home. Had it been in vain?

As he meditated he heard the sound of the young Christians singing,

'To the world I say, "No," I accept the cross – for ever.'
Well over a hundred young people won from Islam had

been present in the camps that year. There had been more than twenty conversions in that one camp. To see their sincerity, to hear their ardent prayers, to realise their tremendous courage in returning to their homes determined to face the blows and the whippings, to remain faithful to their Lord. Truly the Lord had fulfilled the promise. It was almost too good to be true, almost incredible, yet it was true. He dropped to his knees and wept tears of joy as he thanked God for His faithfulness. Truly there is nothing too hard for God.

He had helped these young people as they studied the epistle to the Galatians, and found that it applied so aptly to their problems. They had discovered and appropriated the promise, 'If you are Christ's then you are Abraham's offspring, and heirs according to promise.' Faced with an impossible situation, Abraham had by his own efforts produced Ishmael. He was born according to the flesh. These young folk were from Muslim homes. They were by nature the descendants of Ishmael. From their youth they had been taught to follow a religion of works. The condemnation of God on Ishmael was, 'Cast out the bondwoman and her son.' It had struck home to the hearts of these young Muslims. But when Abraham was a hundred years old, the promise had been renewed to him, 'Sarah your wife shall have a son.' Sarah had laughed in unbelief, but the Lord said to Abraham, 'Is anything too hard for God? Sarah shall have a son.' Abraham trusted God's Word. The Lord visited Sarah as He had said. The miracle had taken place, and the promised son was born. Nothing is too hard for God. These young people, the descendants of Ishmael, had studied the Word of God, the precious Seed had penetrated their hearts, they had believed and the miracle of the new birth had taken place in them. They were now the children of Abraham. No one could stop that work of God. Ishmael might persecute Isaac, as the descendants of Ishmael were persecuting them but Isaac was the true child of Abraham and they were true children of God. Nothing is too hard for God.

Many years later God told Jeremiah to purchase a field in a land which he knew would shortly be dominated and possessed by the King of Babylon. The people would go into captivity, their land would be laid waste, but the promise of God was, 'Houses and fields and vineyards shall again be bought in this land.' It seemed incredible, but in faith Jeremiah obeyed and, as he knelt in prayer, he said, 'Ah! Lord God! behold thou hast made the heaven and the earth by thy great power and thy stretched out arm, and there is nothing too hard for thee.' When Jeremiah realised this tremendous truth, when in obedience, he acted upon it, then God gave this assurance to his faithful servant, 'Behold I am the Lord, the God of all flesh. Is there anything too hard for me?' Has not this passage a very pertinent spiritual application to the closed land of Algeria today? The enemy of souls seems to have triumphed, but a spiritual triumph will yet be won in that hard land. What a fool Jeremiah appeared to be to the men of his day and age! Yet he dared to believe God. The men and women who, acting upon the command of the Lord, counting on His faithfulness, go out to Muslim lands are fools in the eyes of men. Yet today our God is the God of Abraham, the God of Jeremiah. There is nothing too hard for God!

Hard indeed must be the heart of the Christian who can read of the faith and courage of young Algerian Christians without being challenged. An even greater challenge came from an Algerian Muslim. Wistfully he had listened to the gospel message for the first time.

'What wonderful words!' he said to Abd alMasih. 'Are there many others besides yourself who know this?'

'Indeed there are, for there are millions in the world who have believed in Jesus Christ and through Him have found peace and joy and forgiveness.'

'But surely no one else in this land knows it?'

'Oh yes, they do.'

'How many others know it?'

'There must be many in Algiers alone and many, many more in Europe.'

'Then, if they really believe it, why has no one ever been to tell us? No, you Christians do not really believe your message. If you did really believe you would have come to us before!'

Thus this ignorant Muslim youth, with wonderful acumen and insight, pinpointed the reason for the non-evangelisation of Muslims. Unbelief. 'You do not really believe, or you would have come to us long ago?' The words pierced Abd alMasih's heart like a sword. He looked across the hills of Kabylia to the sea. Half a million unevangelised Muslims! He and Lalla Jouhra had determined that, by the grace of God, they would do all that they could to show these people that they really did believe, and care. Yet what could two Christian missionaries accomplish among half a million Muslims?

The paucity of spiritual results in Muslim work must in large measure be placed at the door of unbelieving Christians. 'He could there do no mighty work – because of their unbelief.' Unbelief limits the power of God. The background of this book has been the land of Algeria, for the writer is well acquainted with that land, but the challenge applies equally to every Muslim country. Many were convinced that in independent Algeria all gospel activity would cease, but God has His ways of working. He is the God of the impossible. Nothing is too hard for Him. As the doors in North Africa close, in the Sovereignty of God, He has prepared nationals to

continue the work. But other Muslim lands are wide open
to the gospel, and the need for workers is great.

A visitor from Europe who first sees a group of Muslims
listening to the Word of God is always tremendously
impressed. 'How they listen! They listen as if their lives
depended on it,' was the comment of one who watched
the rapt attention of Muslim youths to the Christian
message. They are gripped by it. And in a very real way
their lives do depend on this message. Yet, how shall they
hear without a preacher? Satan's lie that Muslims cannot
be evangelised is still propagated and believed by
millions of gullible Christians.

It is still true that the religious leaders oppose the
messengers, but so did the Jews in Paul's day. It is true that
the converts are persecuted and because of the intense
opposition many are driven to become secret believers. In
central Africa where Abd alMasih spent some years of his
life, the convert to Christianity has everything to gain.
Prestige, employment, education and advancement in the
social scale all accompany conversion. In Muslim lands
the convert has everything to lose, perhaps even life itself.
This has contributed to the paucity of outward results
in such lands, but the command still stands, 'Preach the
gospel to every creature.' The Lord included Muslims.
Faith obeys His command. Faith relates the problems to
God. Nothing is too hard for Him.

PRAY the Lord of the harvest that He will send forth
labourers into His harvest. Do we really believe that God
hears and answers believing prayer? To listen to the
ardent prayers of young converts from Islam is a spiritual
tonic. They ask, they believe, they witness, they suffer;
and God works. They believe that nothing is too hard for
God. Do we?

GIVE THEM TO EAT. Unbelief limits and restricts our giving. We shall not give Muslims the Bread of Life if we do not believe that they hunger. The lad trustfully handed over his five small loaves, and the Lord used them. Do we really believe? Faith looks to God and gives. Unbelief withholds and limits God.

GO into all the world. A glance at the Prayer Guide will show a tremendous contrast between the number of workers who go to heathen lands and those who evangelise Muslims. Comparisons are odious, but the contrast remains. Young Algerian Christians believe that there is nothing too hard for God. They witness, they go and tell others and God works through them. The man or woman who does not believe will never go to Muslims. Do we really believe? Faith obeys, faith goes, faith witnesses. Then the God of the impossible works.

Muslims are hard. They are too hard. Too hard for man, really tough, but they are not too hard for God. Be it ours to pray with Jeremiah (32:17), 'Ah, Lord God! Behold thou hast made the heavens and the earth by thy great power and stretched out arm, and THERE IS NOTHING TOO HARD FOR THEE.'

To the fountain

Postscript

Land of the Re-emerging Church

by Daisy Marsh

The Berber language, Kabyle, was no longer heard on Radio Algiers. The authorities were afraid of the youthful zeal of those who rejected Islam, craving a deeper knowledge of the religion of their forefathers – Christianity. Tuning in to Radio Monte Carlo one evening, not only was the voice speaking their language – it was speaking of the very religion they were seeking! It was not the voice – it was the power of God's Word behind the voice that gripped them.

The steady sowing of the Seed of God's Word over many years by faithful servants of God was beginning to bear fruit – at last – in a land considered impossible to evangelise. There is NOTHING TOO HARD FOR GOD!

In 1969, towards the end of sixteen years of missionary service in Algeria, I received a hint that God might be preparing me for radio outreach to the Kabyle people amongst whom I was born and brought up. My aunt, wife of the late Bishop of the Arctic, had spent time with a life-long friend who was a missionary broadcaster to the Berbers of Morocco. 'Has your niece ever thought of broadcasting in Kabyle?' the missionary asked. The thought was passed on, and laid aside, but four years later it began to take on fresh meaning for me.

Meantime I had left Algeria and was seeking God's direction for the future. Whilst visiting in Marseille I was offered all the facilities available at Radio School of the Bible, should God ever call me to radio broadcasting to the Kabyles. There was no outreach to them at this time over the air. So it was towards the end of 1972 God's plan for me unfolded.

Little did I know that during this period, the Kabyle people, Berbers of Algeria, and those principally reached by my parents and grandparents from the beginning of the century, were becoming unsettled. They, as the original people of North Africa, were beginning to rebel against Arab domination. Way back in the time of Augustine and Tertullian, the Berbers were Christian; then the Arabs invaded and forced Islam upon them. Latterly, as further pressure was brought to bear upon this people to conform to Islam and Arab culture, Kabyle youth protested. They formed an underground movement and resisted. The Kabyle language was for some time no longer heard on Radio Algiers, and all Kabyles were forced to speak Arabic in the streets. It was then that many, tuning in to Radio Monte Carlo, a favourite commercial station, heard their language. Surely someone was boosting their cause! This resulted in hundreds of letters of encouragement from those thinking this to be a political move on the part of enthusiasts in France. Slowly, but very definitely, the listeners had to be taught that the kingdom for which we were working was not of this world – it was a spiritual one!

Slowly, but very surely, one after another expressed interest, followed a Bible correspondence course, and came to faith in Christ! All over Kabylia little groups of believers were forming – those who rejected Islam, and were seeking to embrace the religion of their ancestors, yet knowing little or nothing of the meaning of being a disciple of Christ.

A name sometimes given to North Africa in the past was 'Land of the Vanished Church'. But here was a re-emerging church, rising from the Seed sown over many years by those single kernels of wheat, willing to sacrifice their lives to the evangelism of a seemingly unresponsive people. They persisted – faithful to their calling from a God who is Faithful. Their labour was not in vain in the Lord!

One leader of a Christian group in Algeria wrote recently, 'We as a group of 30 believers in our village desire to serve the Lord. We realise we need to grow in our faith so that we may attain spiritual maturity and see the world as God sees it. We want to move ahead in the work of evangelism, but WE NEED HELP! . . .'

Today there are almost no expatriate ambassadors for Christ in Algeria. Back in the 1970s, as I and others prayed that God would prepare a male voice to proclaim the message of the Gospel over the air in Kabyle, He was already answering. Women are so despised in Muslim lands, and it seemed a sign of weakness for only a woman's voice to be heard giving such an important message. God had His purpose even in this at such a time of political unrest, but He was already working in the hearts of two Kabyle men, one of whom had himself come to know the Lord through the radio programmes. Both are proving faithful servants of God in the task He has given to them, and many hearts are being moved to accept Jesus Christ as Lord and Saviour as they listen to the five half-hour programmes each week that go out over Trans-World Radio.

One of these broadcasters has recently taken a bold stand in allowing himself to be seen on satellite television, teaching those young believers in his homeland how they can become faithful and effective witnesses for Christ.

Very shortly the whole Bible is to appear in Kabyle, prepared solely by national believers. The whole of the New

Testament, which has been revised and is in print in bilingual version, has also been transferred onto cassette for the use of those who cannot read.

The 'JESUS' film is being widely used in towns and villages, where sometimes only one television set is available for the population to see the film together. But many are believing as they see the wonderful things done by the Lord Jesus Christ, as well as all He suffered that they might have life. This film, produced by Campus Crusade in the U.S.A., has been dubbed in the Kabyle language by a group of believers who first heard the Gospel over the airwaves – maybe the grandsons and daughters of those who long years ago heard the Gospel from a weary servant of God tramping his way across the Atlas mountains, going from village to village sowing the Seed of God's Word – those whose hearts had been softened by some deed of kindness in the Name of Christ: a tooth pulled, or an aspirin to relieve an aching head, a sympathetic listening ear when a seeker came to seek out God's servant at the dead of night so as to avoid the prying eyes of family and friends opposed to the Gospel.

God's promise stands firm to this day: 'I *will* build my Church, and the gates of Hades will not overcome it.' There is NOTHING TOO HARD FOR GOD, and as the years continue to unfold, I believe that the re-emerging church in North Africa will go from strength to strength according to God's promise.

Let us praise Him for all that is past, and trust Him for all that's to come!

Appendix

Echoes of Service

Some readers may be unfamiliar with Echoes of Service. Echoes has functioned as a missionary service group since 1872, based for most of that time in Bath. It was originally the vision of Dr John Maclean and Henry Groves, whose father Anthony Norris Groves had served as a missionary in Baghdad and subsequently in India. Groves' father is sometimes referred to as the father of faith missions and came from the same church background, the Christian Brethren, as George Muller, his brother in law. Henry Groves' concern was to record the missionary work of those who were serving God in different parts of the world with no formal links to any of the existing missionary societies. They were simply depending on God to guide them in their service and provide for their daily needs.

Since 1872 a monthly missionary magazine has been produced as a focus for news and prayer, and this still remains a central part of Echoes' ministry. Over six thousand missionaries, who have served in nearly one hundred countries, have been associated with Echoes of Service, and this represents the largest single Protestant missionary body that has gone out from the UK. The role of Echoes has grown over the years into that of a service group, which receives and transmits monies, provides care and backup for missionaries and seeks to promote world mission. The missionaries are generally from Christian Brethren churches, those from the UK. currently numbering about 380, and are serving in over 45 countries. Similar organisations have developed in other countries; some of these are long standing such as Christian Missions in Many Lands (USA), Missionary Service Committee (Canada), Australian Missionary Tidings (Australia), Missionary Services (New Zealand) and Interlink (Scotland). Newer agencies have emerged in recent years in many countries including Italy, Korea and Malaysia and these represent a truly global outreach.

For further information contact Echoes office at 1 Widcombe Crescent, Bath BA2 6AQ or e-mail us at Echoes_of_Service@compuserve.com

Dr Ian Burness
Echoes of Service, Bath

The passage of thirty years has seen little change in the beliefs held by the Muslim inhabitants of rural villages in North Africa and other parts of the world, and Charles Marsh's classic work 'Share Your Faith With A Muslim' is probably still the best practical manual for work among such people. It shows how he succeeded in making the Gospel of Christ a living reality to them and is certainly due for a reprint in the near future. (Charles Marsh: *Share Your Faith With A Muslim*, Moody Press, o/p)

More recently, Daisy Marsh has written her own fascinating autobiography. Speaking fluent Kabyle since childhood, she has had wonderful opportunities to share the love of Christ with a generation torn by religious fanaticism, political hatred, cruelty, bloodshed, and strife. Many, searching for a better way, have now found it in Christ the Light of the World. (Daisy Marsh: *There's a God in Heaven*, Gazelle Books, 1997)